Remember These Things

by

PAUL HARVEY

With an Introduction by

EDDIE RICKENBACKER

Arrangement by

JOHN M. PRATT

Published by

The Heritage Foundation, Inc.

75 East Wacker Drive, Chicago 1, Ill.

DISTRIBUTED BY GARDEN CITY BOOKS

Garden City, New York

Remember These Things

This book records strains and stresses, doubts and uncertainties such as were never known, on such a scale, since men first trod the surface of the earth.

It is permeated by faith in our divine origin and our ultimate destiny; understanding of our constant dependence on spiritual guidance and under-pinning that are the first essentials to our survival as a nation. On page 42 we find:

> "But there are green years . . . new frontiers . . . for America's new pioneers . . . if we can just revive that wonderful land which once was . . . where any man willing to stay on his toes could reach for the stars."

The author of REMEMBER THESE THINGS, Paul Harvey, literally "grew up" with radio and matured in the atmosphere of television. He has a regular following that is numbered by millions of people.

Paul Harvey is unique among news commentators and radio broadcasters in that the American Legion at its 34th National Convention presented him with its first National Award for "militant Americanism and outstanding broadcasts."

History is the record of events which fashion the lives of men and the destinies of nations. In a very real sense Paul Harvey is an historian. He makes of record current happenings throughout the whole world that become factors in shaping political and economic decisions which determine the pattern of things to come.

Constantly scanning the content of world-wide news dispatches and through experience and native ability, which enable him to understand their meaning, Paul Harvey, with unqualified conviction, great simplicity, a rare facility of expression and convincing eloquence, makes a spoken record for posterity.

This book is offered as an instrument to aid in maintaining and strengthening the framework of America's Priceless Heritage—its free institutions.

We acknowledge, with appreciation, our indebtedness to The Burton-Dixie Corporation for permission to use the texts of Paul Harvey's radio broadcasts some of which are quoted in REMEMBER THESE THINGS.

John M. Pratt, for
The Publishers

INTRODUCTION

By
Eddie Rickenbacker

Not since our forefathers wrote the Declaration of Independence and the Constitution of these United States of America has any author portrayed their true meaning to the extent that my good friend—Paul Harvey—has in REMEMBER THESE THINGS.

In it, Paul Harvey reveals the wisdom and justice of our forefathers and their appreciation of the weaknesses and failures of human beings.

REMEMBER THESE THINGS makes us vividly conscious of how little we, of this generation, remember of what we have been or what we have known. One of the great weaknesses of human beings is our failure to remember in proper perspective the achievements of our past and thereby we penalize the generations to come.

The Freedoms and Liberties, handed down to us, have made it possible for America to grow into world leadership in the short period of 165 years. Without these freedoms and opportunities, we Americans might now be paying the penalty that the peoples of practically every other nation in the world are paying today—namely, being slaves of the State, instead of the State being a servant of the people.

The clamor for material security is one of the greatest subterfuges ever imposed on a people by dishonest government officials who have let themselves be influenced by tumbleweed thinkers from all parts of the world where misery and poverty are commonplace and slavery the accepted order. This book shows when and how we traded real opportunity for imagined security.

To me, one of the greatest words in the English dictionary today is the word FAILURE. One of the greatest privileges that we of this New World can enjoy, regardless, is the privilege to fail, because freedom to fail implies freedom to succeed.

If we had a few million more men like Paul Harvey in this great country of ours we would have no fear for America's future and man's freedom. REMEMBER THESE THINGS is as near to the spirit of the New Testament, insofar as Americans are concerned, as anything that has ever come to my attention.

It is my firm belief that a copy of REMEMBER THESE THINGS should be placed in every public school, every high school and every college in this great land of ours. It should become "must" reading for all boys and girls over ten years of age.

Eddie Rickenbacker

REMEMBER THESE THINGS

CONTENTS

Remember These Things

CHAPTER I

How It Began

TRIP TO WASHINGTON

You've been ganged-up on right here at the start.

A couple of cow farmers out where the grass meets the ground have something to say.

You've heard me mention Farmer Brown from Honey Creek.

Tom Brown and Paul Harvey are neighbors only as they happen to share a state line and talk the same language. I mean mostly two-syllable words.

What we have to say is in that kind of words. Unsorted. Some are Tom's; some are mine.

Farmer Brown and I were in Washington a few days back.

We saw a building called "Commerce." From "E" to Constitution and a whole block wide and a niche every forty feet where a thief can hide . . .

A building called "Justice" . . . outside it says, "The Hall of Justice is a Hallowed Place." . . . Not exactly what the newspapers say.

A labyrinth of corridors called "State" . . . And no states-men. Once white stone, indelibly stained now.

The Supreme Court, a place of quiet Corinthian dignity, where the lean young traitor walked in with stolen secrets in his briefcase and walked out with a character reference.

We saw the Pentagon—five-sided temple to Mars which, for as long as time, will be one dimension out of square.

And there, spanning with our eyes the marble and lime-stone tombstones to honor . . . long since buried . . . up toward Arlington where a hundred-thousand Custers sleep . . . we might have wept.

Except, such times, we get so gol durned mad!

The cost!

The frightful waste!

The corruption!

The black shame of it which makes honest men want to hide their eyes!

When again will decent folks rise up and find the spirit for a hanging!

That's what Americans used to do when they caught the sheriff conniving with the cattle rustlers. People figured with that going on no man's property was safe.

In Dead Man's Hollow the law and the lawless were strung up on the same limb.

I want to tell you something about these buildings and what they once stood for.

Once upon a time some men got together.

They were scared.

Fear bunched 'em.

They were not cowards. You'll see that in a minute.

And they were not second-raters . . . Not men of failure
and frustration . . . Not academic theorists.

They were successful men of business and agriculture, but
they were scared. They had interests to protect . . . these
men of thirteen scattered colonies. Their own and the
interests of many other working folks.

They saw a specter which had haunted men since the first
dim morning of organized government . . . the tax man's
stranglehold on freedom. Always up to that day in 1776
A.D. the ruler's tax man had stood at the citizen's elbow to
snatch away all but subsistence . . . or less.

To keep the ruler fat.

To give the ruler a mansion, refurbished, refurnished, and
with bulletproof windows. To give the ruler a summer
place in the shade and a winter place in the sun and an
income of his own . . . untaxed.

Don't you make out I'm saying something here I'm not.

We're talking about what once was. Taxes . . . more and
more . . . to support more and more of the ruler's favored
ones.

Someone near the throne would now and again toss a few
crusts to the cash contributor. Show him something for his

money. A gift, a jackpot, a circus. A parity, a pension, a dam or hospital annex. A pamphlet, revised.

And armies and ships of war for "protection."

And so the taxpayer bought what he thought was protection. Only the rulers always came back later anyway . . . for his sons.

So these farmers and businessmen in 1776 said,

"No more of that."

They looked across the seas and said we'll not support forever a hereditary English crown and the trappings of the English Court and the commissions of ten thousand tax collectors.

Colonists North and South wrangled for weeks . . . months. Each had brought his own sectional pet dog and pork barrel to the councils. They almost broke up a hundred times.

But they didn't.

Because always the thought of that Red Coated tax collector eating off the little woman's kitchen table did the trick.

In fear they came together . . . and stayed.

Nor could tyranny backed by the military stop them now.

They wrote and signed a Declaration of Independence, pledging their lives, their fortunes, and their sacred honor.

Puritan North . . . Aristocratic South . . . And they fought for that declaration, and some died. Then . . . they got together again.

They wrangled some more.

And they wrote a charter to limit the scope and tenure of the rulers to come.

They purposely limited Federal power. They'd had enough of big government. They wanted little government . . . big people.

And with freedom in their hearts and an old buckskin shirt on their backs they headed off over the mountains.

There was no TVA out there . . . no price supports . . . no price control . . . no job for sure . . . no guaranteed rocking chair. Just liberty, justice, equality and a patch of earth to spade.

And yet those freedom-loving men sang out so loud the glories of this situation that all the oppressed of all the earth looked on and envied.

And these United States of America became something worth a life's sacrifice . . . just to travel toward.

It's 1776 again. Right now!

We, tonight, are taxed to feed and fatten a court of two and a half million federal payrollers and their families.

And what's worse, we're right back supporting British royalty, the British navy, and the decaying remnants of the British Empire *and half the world* besides!

Once more the Red Coats are eating off the kitchen table.

Yes, it's 1776 again. And it's time for another Boston Tea Party.

And we have another bunch of men who are scared. They're not cowards. They're just farmers and business-men who DON'T WANT TO GO BACK!

Pint-sized tyrants began by controlling things . . . ended up controlling people.

They've been freezing this freedom and freezing that free-dom. They've been inching an economic ice cap over us for twenty years now.

We're cold and we're scared and a man can get dis-couraged. But we're going to get mad, instead!

And as long as we're forked end down we aim to fight.

Now hear this . . . for all their slum-born vote-getting machines they will not buy out Honey Creek and Kokomo.

We want a new Declaration of Independence. Telling that man he can NOT take over the free businesses and the free press and the free labor of free men no matter what he thinks.

And cut out the free feed for the boss hogs at the public trough and the spill-over they've been leaving us. We'll manage.

Call in this stage money and give us back a dollar we can bite and we'll buy our own bread and our own insurance and have money left over.

We in Illinois and Wisconsin and South Carolina and Georgia and North Dakota will not let our old, our poor, our insane and our misfits starve or lack shelter. Nor will we let labor be hijacked by ruthless employers. We will not.

And when the farm dole stops, we won't stop farming. We'll go right on putting seed in the ground and hay in the barn and corn in the silo and milk in the can.

And we'll swap overalls for tractor parts until new leadership puts some cents back in our dollar.

Yokes, hobbles, and halters were not meant for humans.

Government has to be cut back like asparagus . . . every day . . . or it gets away and goes to seed. Ours did. When there's too much of it, the flower becomes a weed.

You name one legitimate function of government . . . law and order . . . or you name any American objective dealing with real welfare . . . and we'll find some way to do it without help from any other state.

Word's going around the country . . . and there's still lots of country in this country . . .

Cattle men of Kansas, corn-hog men of Iowa, housewives of Indiana, stalwarts of Texas . . . It's 1776 again.

Scared Americans are whooping it up for some inalienable rights that got misplaced somewhere back there. You stick around . . . Government "of the people" is going to mean something again.

COMMUNISM IN NEW ENGLAND

The Pilgrim Fathers of the United States were communists.

The self-government which they established in Massachusetts was communistic.

All that they owned and all the crops which they grew became the common property of all. A man's task was assigned him by central authority. Food was rationed. At first a quarter-pound of bread a day to each person.

Some of the Pilgrims complained that they were too weak from want of food to tend the crops as they should. There was increasing absenteeism.

"So," writes Governor Bradford, "the colonists began to think how they might raise as much corn as they could and obtain a better crop than they had done."

At last, in 1623, after much debate, the governor, with the advice of the chief of the colonists, decided upon a *new* system whereby each man should plant his own corn. Each would therefore have to trust himself for the food for his family.

Each family was assigned a parcel of land. Governor Bradford said, "This had very good success, for it made all hands very industrious so as much more corn was planted."

They now went willingly into the field and took their little ones with them to set corn.

Before, they would have alleged weakness and inability to work. To have compelled them to work would have been tyranny. But now they worked willingly.

By the time the next harvest had come, instead of famine there was plenty. The effect of the private planting was apparent to all. Some of the more industrious had to spare, and to sell to others.

"So," wrote Governor Bradford, "any general want or famine has not been amongst them to this day."

The communist experiment in America—as with all communist experiments past, present, and future—was foredoomed to failure.

Our new system of government was based on First Corinthians 3:8: "Every man shall receive his own reward according to his own labor."

In but a few years free men raised themselves and their society to a pinnacle of progress unapproached in all the ages.

When America's early pioneers first turned their eyes toward the West they did not demand that somebody take care of them if they got ill or got old. They did not demand maximum pay for minimum work, and even pay for no work at all. Come to think of it, they did not demand much of anything—except freedom.

They looked out at those rolling plains stretching away to the tall, green mountains, then lifted their eyes to the blue skies and said, "Thank you, God. I can take it from here."

This nation was not carved out of the wilderness, as some say.

It was scratched and chopped and dug and plowed and hammered and clawed out.

No government in history ever *gave* its citizens what hardworking Americans with their sleeves rolled up, have *earned* for themselves.

Our citizens stood on their own feet and asked nothing for nothing and elected leaders to match.

There was poverty, but there was opportunity. There were hardships, but there was hope. There was security.

Here, at last, was the security men had sought for six thousand years.

A land in which a man was entitled to all the prerogatives of a man.

He set his own limitations.

Nobody else did.

He could climb as high as he could carry his own weight.

Because he got wherever he was under his own steam, he was secure.

Some failed and failed to rise again. So there were poorhouses, as well as mansions. That was the important part. The difference between this nation and the world's older ones being that here the only things which prevented the man in the poorhouse from living in the mansion were his own limitations.

Not because society decreed all men must live in the same category.

One hundred and fifty years ago, the United States was a contemptuously disregarded political experiment on the wrong side of the Atlantic.

Today we are the most prosperous nation on earth. Today, we, seven per cent of the world's people, enjoy more than half the world's good things. All this in one hundred and fifty years!

And the economic vehicle we rode to the top is free competitive American capitalism!

Do not let the word "Capitalism" frighten you. It has been abused, misused, and maligned and slurred like some naughty word nice people do not use . . . but capitalism has been our good servant. Yet some want to trade a good servant for a bad master.

Today we must decide whether the economy which made us great shall be continued or abandoned. Or, and it amounts to the same thing, be modified beyond recognition. The whole world awaits our decision.

Why should we change? When the car is running, why tamper with the carburetor? Matthew 9:12: "They that be whole need not a physician, but they that are sick."

Change has been good as mankind sought to improve his lot. There still must be more change in the imperfect treatment of disease, but *there is no need to change a good wife or a good economic system* of the sort men sought for centuries.

We should tell the quick-change Charlies that we have found what we want. We do not want it switched, watered down, or klobbered up by subversive crooks or restless fools.

I suggest that we profit from history. How stupid can we be . . . to keep making the same identical mistakes over and over again for six thousand years.

Patrick Henry said: "I have but one lamp by which my feet are guided, and that is the lamp of experience. I know of no way of judging the future but by the past."

This is the past. We have gone in circles for six thousand years. The pattern has never changed. From Priest to King, from King to Oligarchy, from Oligarchy to Despot, from Despot to Majority, from Majority to Bureaucracy, from Bureaucracy to Dictator, from Dictator back to King and all over again.

For six thousand years men have gone in circles.

THE VITAL EQUATION

The largest doors in the world are on the Archives Building in Washington, D. C. They are solid bronze and forty-nine feet high.

But too few pass through them.

On the Archives Building, on the stone shoulders of the steps facing Constitution Avenue, are eight words.

On one side it says, "What is past is prologue."

On the other side, "Study the past."

A Washington cab driver is said to have translated their meaning for a tourist: "Mister, that means you ain't seen nothin' yet."

Less succinctly, study how we got where we are if you want to know where we are going.

A Britisher whose name you know has said that the United States will go the way of Rome.

Here are his exact words: "Your Republic," he's speaking to the United States . . . "Your Republic will be pillaged and ravished in the twentieth century just as the Roman Empire was by the barbarians in the fifth century—with this difference:

The devastators of the Roman Empire, the Huns and the Vandals, came from abroad, while your barbarians will be the people in your own country and the product of your own institutions."

Lord Macaulay said that . . . more than a hundred years ago.

He was an historian. An historian knows the basic formula:

MAN + FEAR − GOD = MAN OVER MAN

Deeper in "The Lays of Ancient Rome" he wrote of how it happened . . . and would again. How the Roman provinces were drained dry by excessive and disproportionate taxation levied to support a top-heavy army and a court of political lackeys who stole the people blind.

And how Rome's policy of appeasement allowed the Huns to take over.

Quintus Fabius Maximus thought he could wage a cold war against Hannibal . . . the second Punic War.

The Romans nicknamed Fabius, "Cunctator," meaning "one who delays." While he stalled, the indecisive stalemate soon cost more than war.

Rome was deliberately baited into dissipating its waning strength. Not invaded. The Romans weren't chased out or strung up or shot down. They were worried to death.

Fear drove them to economic suicide.

Analyzing this, Lord Macaulay could tell us where we were going a hundred years before we got there. And that "barbarians . . . from our own institutions" would lead the way.

We are rightly afraid.

But we are afraid of the wrong things.

The history of Rome could be written on the front page and passed off as today's news. In our advanced state of political paranoia we are again paying blackmail to the Huns and Vandals of Asia. Trying to buy away the shadows.

So morally bankrupt ourselves that we cannot lead by example, we try to bribe the world with dollars. Forcing funds and guns on reluctant friends . . . because we are afraid.

Though a proverb as old as Persia says it: "I have taught no one the art of the bow who did not in the end make me his target."

We don't call it fear. We have all sorts of plausible, clever excuses for what we do.

Like the alcoholic who drinks on a cold day to keep warm and on a warm day to cool off and drinks, when he's unhappy, to forget . . . and when he's happy to celebrate.

Anything to dodge the humiliating truth that he is afraid.

We are not the first.

Often Jesus was called upon to counsel, "Fear not. Be not over anxious."

On that last night in the upper room He said, "Let not your heart be troubled, neither let it be afraid."

And so it was in Rome and Spain and Greece and China. Men worked hard, prospered greatly, grew fat, quit work, felt insecure . . . and became afraid.

Afraid of enemies without, they hired more armies.

Afraid of having to go back to work they demanded government guarantees. And failing these and fearing poverty, rattled the cup for handouts. Each great civilization the same.

And what is past is prologue.

Here you and I sit, with all the charts and maps of the past pointing out the right roads and the wrong ones and we, instead of going straight ahead, have to keep turning left, following the same dizzy circle that led these ghost empires of the past into ignominious oblivion—only we're going there six hundred miles an hour.

We are scared sick.

How rare is the political candidate who dares to tell you the whole truth, because the truth is "work or perish" and that is not a very inviting campaign promise. So *they* are afraid, too.

Men comprised of equal components of courage and cowardice negating one another.

Be he Republican or Democrat he knows it's going to cost one hundred billion dollars next year to keep you on this drunken binge and there simply isn't that much money this side of bankruptcy.

The basic conflict is not between the US and the USSR. They are the political manifestations of the battle that really goes on within each of us.

Plato said that each human being is like a rider . . . sitting up on a chariot . . . driving a team of two horses . . . a black one and a white one . . . the good and evil that is in each of us . . . and that the man's job, with the grace of God, is to keep the evil horse from wrecking the chariot.

The businessman is at war within himself. He wants overseas spending to perpetuate the bull market but objects to the high taxes it costs.

The farmer objects to federal spending but not to accepting part of it.

The worker, making a tank for Korea, says a prayer for the boys who will use it; then strikes for higher wages before it is finished.

We all want to buy wholesale and sell retail.

Each of us is two. But, as I say, this is nothing new.

The Apostle Paul said, "Sometimes it seemed I was like two people. I wanted to do one thing and found myself doing another."

And so, Dr. J. Wallace Hamilton says, "Every person is a mixture, a mingling of dust and deity, flesh and spirit, a citizen of two worlds; his heart a battlefield upon which Babylon and the New Jerusalem struggle for mastery.

And every man makes his own heaven or hell, here and hereafter, by what he does with that conflict."

This is the composition we call "human nature." And with this known factor the historian can complete the equation which has been proved over and over and over again:

$$MAN + FEAR - GOD = MAN \ OVER \ MAN$$

Always, the weakling will be ruled by the tyrant.

Right down through the center of man's being is a rift of contradiction. Half of him wants to be bad; half of him wants to be good. And nations, too.

I'm not talking political jargonese.

This is no finger-waving in the direction of Washington or Moscow.

This is to say we cannot expect good manners from our children if they never see any. We cannot sell honor and dignity and decency to the rest of the world if we don't have any.

Let's search our own hearts. Americans have explored everything but the explorer.

And study history. Let's analyze how we got this way . . . and why we are so sore afraid.

For centuries men were driven to hysteria by the sun's eclipse. Knowledge cast out that fear.

We may yet get back on this high road . . . and stay there . . . and quit fearing the shapeless shadows of imagined things . . . and act like men again.

I have tried to say it all in an annual Easter message. It's always the same.

This is never the best sermon you hear on Easter, but it's always the shortest:

Jesus lived a good life in a wicked world . . . to show us it could be done. And he died . . . and rose again.

To show us that we could do that, too.

CHAPTER II

Prospects for Tomorrow

You young people might not like what I have to say, but if you remember it that's more important.

Because I am not going to tell you the world is rolling out a red carpet and rolling back all the dark clouds just for you. It is not.

The sooner you learn this the better. Storms are a part of the normal climate of life.

Life is not all ease . . . and it is not all fun for anyone.

In some ways the smarter you are . . . the more it hurts.

But don't worry.

You are not nearly so smart as you think.

A recent New York Times survey showed twenty-five per cent of high school graduates do not know the name of the man who was president of this country during the Civil War.

You can graduate from Yale, Harvard, Princeton, Northwestern and most other private schools and from at least

twenty tax-supported state universities without ever knowing the dates of the War of 1812 or the meaning of "deficit
financing" . . . which in case you do not know is a nice
phrase for describing how your government keeps borrow-
ing from the bartender so as to postpone the hangover.

But what manner of capped and gowned persons are these
who are dragging their feet in the line-up for sheepskins.

Every year I have seen some. Recently more, somehow.

You are worried. You are unhappy. You are sorry for yourself. They want to take away your horizon and hand you
a gun.

Well, I will tell you, son . . . one of the wonderful things
about this Republic of ours is that we can erase some of
our mistakes every four years.

If you don't like the way we have run things up to now,
I can't say I blame you. But you take it from here!

Give it more than we gave it.

I once heard New Zealand's Ambassador Berendsen say,
"Of course we cannot always see where we are going.
But a ship's captain does not stop or turn around because
he cannot see over the horizon. He charts his course and
he knows where he is going whether he can see it or not."

No, you cannot see over the next hill. The day after Dun-
kirk no man could see victory . . . yet no man doubted
it!

It has always been that way, son.

There is rain *every* Spring.

Now when the storm strikes a rooster, he folds up. Wraps his wings about him for what little protection they afford and just droops. Maybe he gets wet and sick and dies.

When a storm strikes an eagle . . . you know what he does? He spreads his wings and rides the winds until they carry him high above the storm to where he's soaring in the sunshine.

Storms are part of the normal climate of life.

Ride 'em!

"But where is opportunity?" I hear the cynic say.

"Where is there a chance for the Henry Fords and the Horatio Algers in this era of regulation and regimentation?"

Son, look up.

Just look up! Why we have sent a message to the moon and got it back. At 186 thousand miles a second we bounced a message off the moon! What is it good for? I don't know. No one told Henry Ford what to do with the principle of internal combustion.

Where's opportunity today?

For the purpose of illuminating our airlift airfields in Berlin at night . . . Westinghouse developed a light half as bright as the sun and the size of a cigarette.

Speaking of lights! There is ready for market a kitchen light that not only lights the kitchen but heats the kitchen. It deodorizes the kitchen, drives mosquitoes away, kills all the bacteria in the air, and gives the housewife a suntan at the same time.

We have perfected sound anesthesia. I do not mean "knocking one's self out on Dorsey's trombone," as the bobby soxers say—but focusing ultra-high-frequency sound on a given area of the human anatomy and effecting total anesthesia with absolutely no ill after affects.

Detroit is experimenting with a stretch of heated highway which will clear itself of snow at a fraction of the cost of the old sweat shovel and swear way.

You asked where is opportunity today!

The Air Force and the Atomic Energy Commission have completed the first phase in the development of an atom powered airplane designed to circle the earth eighty times on one pound of fuel.

Dr. Allen Dumont sees intercontinental telecasting by 1960.

Maybe there is the ultimate answer to world peace. For though languages differ all over the earth, all laughter and all pain sound the same. Maybe when we can hear alike and see alike we will come to think alike and realize our common objectives.

General Electric has designed an electric helmsman which means a ship may be steered from any place on board.

Temple University has come up with a torch, a tiny blue flame hotter than 9000 degrees Fahrenheit. That is as hot as the surface of the sun.

Where is opportunity today?

We have caught up with the comic strips. A wrist radio with no wires, no batteries. Powered by 45 seconds exposure to sunlight it runs for 48 hours. A wrist radio . . . so that Dad can call home in the evening and explain that he is unavoidably detained at the office without ever putting down his poker hand.

Once there was a farmer . . . who decided to sell his farm. Figured he would get another more to his liking.

He called in a real estate man and listed the farm for sale. The real estate man said all right. He prepared an ad for the papers. When it was finished, he proofread it to the farmer.

The ad described the farm's advantages, ideal location, handy roads, good fences, fertile acres, well-bred stock, plenty of water.

"Wait a minute," said the farmer. "Read that again."

The real estate man read it again . . .

"Handy roads, good fences, fertile acres, well-bred stock, plenty of water . . ."

The farmer said, "Stop right there. It is not for sale."

The real estate man asked why the sudden change of heart and the farmer replied, "That is just the sort of place I have been looking for all my life."

There it is, graduates . . .

All I have tried to do is to write up the ad . . . for the great future you have inherited . . . in the great nation we have come to take for granted.

You hear your elders . . . me included, sometimes . . .
so emphasize what is wrong with our wonderful land that
we unintentionally minimize what is right.

Where is there another Edison or George Washington Carver or the many men for the million minor miracles that
await?

Who is going to finish that platform for which some federal funds already have been appropriated . . . a platform to be erected in outer space seven tenths of the way
to the moon?

In a way it is unfair to measure the opportunities in America solely in terms of scientific advance . . .

But you students so often do . . .

You don't want me to tell you what Thomas Jefferson or
Dan Webster said. You want to know what would they
say today.

Well, I think they would say . . . "look up!"

There have been wars, depressions, and problems for every
generation.

They would say, "We rode out some storms . . . in our
time, too."

And now . . .

There are new horizons, new frontiers, for America's new
pioneers, more limitless than they have ever been.

Opportunity today is as exciting as flying saucers . . .

As potentially powerful as the unharnessed atom . . .

And as vast as the Milky Way.

Young Americans, you stand on the threshold of the most fascinating era in the history of the world.

FACING THE FACTS

In view of our technical accomplishments it is understandable that we should consider ourselves quite clever.

But unfortunately that is not all egoism implies.

The egoist comes to think . . . not just that he is smarter than his fellow man . . . but that he is smarter than God.

Let's face it.

Man never invented anything.

All the brains of the Massachusetts Institute of Technology, Bell Laboratories and General Electric and our institutes of aeronautical research have never invented anything.

We just "discovered" certain things.

The elements of electricity and radio and television and jet-propulsion . . . all have been here since the beginning of time. But for each generation the curtain was parted a little further to reveal more of those things that were there all along.

The mysteries of creation have been revealed to us only according to our capacity to absorb and utilize.

Once upon a time there was a man named Moses.

A leader of men.

One day he pitched camp at a place called Meribah.

But there was no water for his people.

Moses said, "What shall I do, Lord?"

The Lord commanded Moses to strike a rock with a stick and there came forth great quantities of water from the rock.

In effect Moses said, "Look what I did!"

God said, "Shame on you, Moses. Rather than glorify me before your people you glorify yourself."

So, for his egoism, Moses was punished . . . by being permitted to see over into the Promised Land . . . but never to enter.

In the early 1930's Samuel Insull announced to a meeting of his directors, "I now control all electricity in Illinois and Indiana . . ."

Listen to his words carefully. Electricity, he thought, belonged to him.

Then he inserted a profane phrase and added, "I now propose to control all transportation too!" Approximately six months later . . . Sam Insull, disguised in women's clothing, was in an open boat in the Aegean Sea fleeing an extradition warrant.

History is studded with stories of egoism which, more than any other vice or weakness, has caused so many to fall.

Alexander the Great, Sampson, the cruel kings and queens of England, Napoleon, the Kaiser and Hitler and now Stalin!

But let us watch our own step, too.

The curtain has been parted for us more than for any other people.

Therefore, the responsibility is multiplied proportionately.

Whether our new discoveries shall be used for good or for evil is entirely up to us.

I do not like some of the signs I see.

The indolent content to be parasites on the industrious.

Adolescents imitating the standards of their parents' favorite night club comedian.

Immorality of our citizens in turn spawning corruption in our government.

And men claiming personal credit for the bountiful "waters of Meribah."

Look out!

Pride goeth before a fall.

There have been great civilizations before ours. Others sought out some of the secrets of the infinite.

But they were trusted with more knowledge than they would rightly employ . . . and so it was taken from them.

Here, in the United States, for the first time in six thousand years . . . a new experiment in government was founded because men sought freedom to worship.

It prospered because they did.

Then somehow we forgot why.

Instead of, "What hath God wrought?" we said, "Look what I did!"

Our pride and arrogance aroused jealous enemies to hate and attack us.

THE PROMISED LAND

Mankind searched for six thousand years; then . . .

In 1787 with the signing of our Constitution there was born the first government of, by, and for the *people* . . . and based on *individual* freedom and *voluntary* cooperation . . . under the laws of God.

We found the Promised Land!

Now a lot of lisping nincompoops want to get us back in that ridiculous rut and head us for that same graveyard of empires through representing what they are recommending, as progress.

Let them not alter the label on the poison bottle.

Let them call it "necessary," but let them not call it "new."

Let them call it "expedient," but let them not call it "progress."

Let them say we no longer deserve the right to think and act for ourselves.

But let them not say that this is to preserve our "freedom."

Income taxes are not new.

The first income tax was paid by Abraham. A subsequent one was written on a rock by the hand of Divinity and given to Moses at the top of Mount Sinai. It was at the flat rate of ten per cent.

At Runnymede the Magna Charta was handed to King John on the end of a sword . . . denying to royalty the right of unlimited taxation.

But, it was for the American people to become the first ever voluntarily to return that tyrannical power to government.

Then, in 1932, the next big step backward was taken. What had been a government of, by, and for the people . . . became instead a government *of* executive directors and bureaus *by* appointees having the power to make rules with the force of law and the power to construe those rules and to enforce them.

All the powers any king in history ever had . . . were handed to men not even duly elected.

Such was called a "new" deal.

Finally, recently, the United States prepared once more in the pattern of the first confused, frightened Pilgrims . . . to ration food, to allocate farm crops by decree, to regulate what could be sold and to whom and for how much.

To regulate where a man should work and at what wage.

To remove further limitless amounts from his wage in taxes.

We allowed ourselves to be convinced that we were not wise enough to manage our own affairs, that we should let the government do it for us.

We allowed ourselves to be deluded that this was the way to a new order of things . . . to make over God's world with no hills . . . no valleys . . . all level.

Is it possible that the American people will awaken in their comfortable parlor-car seats, look out the window, and realize in time that somewhere back there the Freedom Train got off the track?

That we switched off the main line and turned left?

Could it be that we may yet shake off the leg iron someone locked on while we slept and seek out the engineer and demand . . . with the courage of bare-handed men . . . that he get us back on the high road?

Serve notice we are not going to be wrecked or returned to serfdom by our own frock-coated crew!

If we all left the parlor car and got back to competing to see who could shovel the most coal nobody could even catch, much less wreck, this train.

Then the American historians of some distant tomorrow might write, as Governor Bradford wrote, "Any general want or famine has not been amongst them to this day." Could it be . . . ?

But free men . . . free to do anything . . . are also free to do nothing.

Apparently that is our choice.

We said we no longer wanted "opportunity."

We wanted "security."

And they gave us chains.

And we were secure.

When some future Gibbon writes "The Decline and Fall of the American Republic" . . . let him be honest.

Let him say the great new system of government called free competitive American capitalism brought forth such bountiful harvest of all good things . . . that the people . . . grown fat . . . grew lazy.

Their leaders, instead of destroying their enemies, copied them.

And history's shining hour came to an end.

FREEDOM HAS FOUR WHEELS

One day in Philadelphia in 1778, for the first time in the history of the world, men of experience blueprinted the Republic. There began the world's first great era of governmental progress.

What was their formula? It was a written contract called the Constitution, which established four units. It provided for the authority of a President, a Congress, a Court, *and the individual*. It guaranteed that no one could run away with the others.

Every tyranny in history has had a short life; and, as
James Madison said, every democracy has died a violent
death.

But here was a Republic—a government which governs
neither too little nor too much.

It provided that one man, in the interests of others, may
be told what "not" to do. But it does not tell him what
"to" do.

He may work or quit, pray or not, say what he thinks, and
it is nobody's business but his own.

No government ever before had secured for its people
religious freedom, civil liberty, freedom of speech and
press, security of individual rights or popular education
or universal franchise.

Here, in the words of a sacred compact, was a government
of moderation.

Like a race horse, not completely unharnessed, but with
a limp rein, we spurted forward.

We the People of the United States took a world of ox
carts and put it on wheels of steel and powered the new
world with steam and electricity and gasoline.

Men were free.

Nothing could stop them.

And so it was that Henry Esterbrook said, "I would fight
for every line in the Constitution as I would fight for every
star in the flag."

Then something happened.

We had begun to radiate this great new gospel of government all over the world.

Just as surely as other good things had been copied, good government was being imitated.

The idea of being married to only one woman at a time was first evolved in some country and when the world recognized that it was better than either polygamy or promiscuity it met with almost universal adoption.

The clock was first evolved in some country and when the world recognized the twelve-hour day as the best means of telling the recording time, it met with universal adoption.

And so with weights and measures and the fish-shaped boat. For land travel, men who had experimented with one and two and three and six and eight finally agreed—universally—that the four-wheeled vehicle was the most efficient.

In government, mankind was copying us. From all over the earth men were beginning to lay down their burdens on this new altar of liberty.

Here was a goverment, evolved through reason and experiment and tested by experience and demonstration, and by every standard, it proved it worked best.

Sometimes we like to think we are rich because we have worked harder.

Hard work is not new. The Apostle Paul once cautioned the Romans to be "not slothful in business." The galley slaves and peasant farmers and shopkeepers of the old world had worked hard.

But as a plow horse under the whip, not as a race horse free to run!

So, after seven thousand years of experimental failures, we held aloft for all the world to see the fruits of a Republic—a government that worked!

Then one day, while we were not watching, selfish politicians began to lend-lease our freedom away.

Jealous neighbors and foolish friends began to talk about democracy. Political democracy! Ancient mob rule!

Socially our principles are democratic, but politically we are a Republic. To spoil it, the enemies knew that all they had to do was push it off balance.

Do we have to see our flag trampled by an unharnessed mob or must we get smashed in the teeth by some dictator's musket before we can see what we have lost?

There is no such thing as fractional freedom.

A man is not free when he has even one foot in a bear trap. We have left too many freedoms at the international hock shop already and if we do not redeem them it does not make any difference whether we win or lose in Korea.

No difference at all.

We have strayed a long way from the principles of the men who blueprinted our Republic and who warned us to avoid entangling alliances.

Who cautioned that we should love our neighbors but keep our hedges high, who knew that inheriting a Republic was like inheriting any other kind of riches; it is hard to hang onto it!

We must rededicate ourselves to individual liberty and opportunity. We must rally behind the battle cry of "Back to the Constitution!"

For the Constitution of the United States is a sacred compact binding the dead, the living, and the yet unborn . . . signed in the snow of Valley Forge . . . sealed with the blood of Fort Sumter.

So that men no bigger than you and I might be free.

Once upon a time, in a land afar off, a lad asked his father for money, tied a knapsack on a stick and started off whistling down the road.

He was free. Free of work, worry, stuffy conventions, stodgy religion . . . free. Not a care in the world.

He went to town and had himself a time. He burned his bankroll at both ends.

Until, broke, he had to go to work . . . got a job on a farm.

One day so hungry he ate of the stuff he was feeding the pigs, he said to himself, "Enough of this!" And he headed home to dad.

In the fifteenth verse of Luke he is quoted as saying, "Father, I am no more worthy to be called thy son; make me as one of thy hired servants."

The lad who had had freedom was ready to be servant.

What has happened?

As a free man, he might have fed the stranger's pigs until he had earned enough to buy a farm for himself.

Instead of that he preferred some guaranteed mediocrity.

Any animal of the forest would fight to the death for its freedom.

But here is this lad who had it . . . did not know how to use it . . . and came running home exclaiming, "Make me a hired hand. It is too hard to be a son."

What I am getting at is that it takes a pretty good man to know what to do with freedom when he gets it.

Here in the New World when the eighteenth century was in its teens men found freedom.

Freedom to work and play, debate, and pray, and they used it.

They leaned into the wind and armed with their shiny, new-found freedoms they wrestled the wilderness for the highest stakes in history.

Then a couple of decades ago some political medicine men started telling us that freedom is not worth the trouble of keeping. "Look how hard you have to work for it," they said.

The pills they peddled were guaranteed to make life all ease . . . all honey and no bees . . . and we bought.

We were ready like the boy at the pig trough to trade our freedom for a place to sleep and a bit of bread.

Just let the government make us hired hands, we said.

We had seen the spirit of the Old World corrode away where men traded liberty for security and lost both . . . until, as the late Jan Christian Smuts said, "even the desire for freedom" was gone.

But still we bought their little pink pills.

Make me a hired man, we said. It is too hard to be a son.

"Men are slaves," said Berdyaev, "because freedom is difficult, slavery is easy."

History is full of people sinking into servitude because they would not face the hard fight to stay free.

So we surrendered all that makes man human—the right to think and venture—for bread and soup and chains.

The mechanized world had become too vast and complicated. We could lessen the struggle by reducing our freedom.

In fatigue and frustration we threw ourselves at the feet of the state and said, "Make me a hired man. It is too hard to be a son."

And you can coast . . . only downhill.

But here is where the pessimists and I part ways. I think all the prodigal son needs is a willow switch applied to the seat of his pants, and he might yet be a man.

Doctor Curt Richter of Johns Hopkins stated that all our oomph comes from our adrenal glands and that laziness is shrinking them. Our ease is sapping the fight out of us.

God answers some prayers "yes" and some "no" because if a father, however loving, did all his son's homework . . . he would ruin the son.

The ancient Greeks had a saying that, "If you want to destroy a man give him everything he wants."

We got to the point where Kipling said all men would be "paid for existing" . . . and rot set in.

Today we are traveling on the same old detour to decay.

There is a high road.

It is uphill . . . but we need the exercise.

We can buy back the last good hope on earth—if we really are willing to go back to work . . .

If we are willing to do without a lot of civil servants and fancy services we cannot afford and really go to work . . . this great government under God could last intact through all the earthly time there is.

In Winchester, Indiana . . . there is a great stone base in the middle of the courthouse lawn.

Atop that base is a Grecian-type lamp.

Some time ago in a ceremony in which all faiths participated . . . they ignited the wick in that lamp.

The inscription on the lamp reads:

> "Behold, friend, you are on hallowed ground,
> For here burns Freedom's Holy Light."

The Winchester plan is to keep it burning . . . always.

It will be a community responsibility.

Each in his turn.

To remind all men that freedom is not permanent . . .

Unless there are enough keepers of the flame.

YOU HAVE A REPUBLIC IF—

An old hermit lived in the mountains of Virginia; he was a wise old man—gifted with that rare insight that some men, though uneducated, acquire through close contact with nature and the God of the garden.

The young boys of the village laughed at the old patriarch. "I know how we can fool him," one said. "I'll take a bird in my hand . . . hold it so he can just peek through my fingers . . . and ask him what it is. When he answers, I'll say, 'Is it dead or alive?' If he guesses it's dead, I'll let it fly away. If he says it's alive . . . I'll crush it."

They found him at the door of his hut.

"Old man," said the lad, "I have a question. What's in my hand?"

"Well, my son, it looks like a bird you've caught."

"Right," said the boy. "Now, is it alive or dead?"

The old man fixed his eyes upon the lad for a long moment, then said: "It is as you will, my son."

After four thousand years, the elusive eagle of individual liberty has been captured and placed in our hands.

Now, it is as we will.

We can crush it to death . . . or starve it . . . and it will die.

Or love it . . . feed it . . . and watch it fly.

It is as we will.

Ben Franklin said, "You have a Republic, if you can keep it."

It is as we will.

Out of the same stuff . . . comes fertilizer to enrich the earth . . . or explosives to destroy it—out of the same stuff.

It is as we will.

The late Fulton Oursler has said it is not easy to be a good citizen in a free country.

Of course it is not. Nothing worthwhile ever is easy.

The President of France said freedom is like bread . . . something you go on earning day by day.

Certainly it is easier to obey orders, to learn passively a doctrine, to conform without protest to outside dictates

. . . than to accept responsibility for self-imposed discipline.

But "either servitude or desertion," says President Auriol, "is abdication of the intellect and of the will."

I am not speaking of the disloyal in our midst.

They are dangerous only because of the lazy loyal.

The good citizens have the bad ones outnumbered . . . but the bad ones are busier.

If the United States ever is destroyed . . . it will not be because of somebody else's bombs . . . but because of our own indifference.

The spirit of freedom is not dead in this country.

It has been ridiculed by the Red medicine men to an extent that it has gone into hiding, but it is not dead.

It has been unsold to our children in our schools and to our workers in our factories and our fields, but since there is a spark left let us breathe new life into it while there is yet time.

I know . . .

So many will neither hear nor heed this warning.

The gravy train is running in three sections and factory whistles are making too much noise.

They figure God will save America, without giving him any good reason why he should.

But there are green years . . . new frontiers . . . for America's new pioneers.

If we can just revive that wonderful land which once was . . . where any man willing to stay on his toes . . . could reach for the stars.

CHAPTER III

Source of Strength

FEET IN THE FURROW

The higher a man's office is in a skyscraper . . . the more
he wishes he had his feet in a furrow. We all want to be
where we are not. That is why we have railroads.

So as often as I can . . . I journey from my headquarters
atop Chicago's great Merchandise Mart and follow my
heart to our farm in the Ozarks.

So I have done this weekend.

After a day of getting my perspective back in focus . . . I
think I know where it was we all lost touch with the truth.

It was when we moved to town . . . and left God behind.

We chopped down the trees and suddenly we were, ourselves, like "cut flowers."

To try to recapture what we had lost . . . we built big-
ness around us.

We poured houses for ourselves out of concrete reinforced
with steel. But still we felt insecure. Because somehow our
hearts had turned to stone, too.

We had built our towers great and strong and permanent
and high . . . but all we had really accomplished was to
obscure the sky.

Back on my hilltop in the Ozarks I knew why Jesus had so
often gone up the mountain to pray, why he summoned
his disciples there when he wanted to be sure they got
something straight.

The trouble is that sometimes a Missourian goes away too
far and stays away too long; no Potomac River boat-ride
ever did for a man what fishing in a backwater slough will
do.

Most of the fellows in Washington want what is best for
all of us.

Most of them are honorable, loyal Americans. The only
reason we end up with a government run by the friends
of Alger Hiss is that they honestly do not know what is
happening.

They just cannot see when they are standing in front of the
spotlight.

Well, I'll tell you something . . .

We can see from here. As good, God-fearing, hard-working
dirt farmers we do not like watching the weeds choke out
the flowers.

Down at Potts Hargrove's General Store . . . they still
give the benefit of the doubt.

They shake their heads and say, half hopefully, you fellows
in Washington must know more about it than we do.

They just will not believe the truth . . . that they are in fact smarter than you.

You figure that you have to buy votes with handouts and promise everybody everything.

It would surprise you to know how many loyal Americans do not expect to be spoon fed by anybody. Twenty years have taught a lot of them to expect pay for doing nothing . . . but not most of them.

Men with their heads in the sun and their fingers in the soil know that not all trees are the same size. That is God's plan and they know why. It makes them all taller trying to outreach each other for the sky.

That is why I say, maybe you fellows in Washington are too far from home . . .

Now my hilltop in the Ozarks is lavender with spring's first Sweet Williams . . . and the birds . . . Red and Blue and Oriole and Bob White . . . hold choir practice in the willow by the sun porch . . .

We are much closer to Korea than the fellows in Washington are.

We would never have deserted Sonny Becker if he had got in trouble back home.

If he had been piled on by a bunch of gangsters back here, there would have been some shooting in these hills.

But over there he is made to get down and wrestle with them . . . all of them.

We drove the jeep down to town. Small Paul loves the jeep . . . you don't miss any of the scenery from a jeep, because you are sitting right out in it.

We were counting the town's six new street lights and detouring around friendly dogs lazing in the warm sun-drenched road, and talking about the boys leaving for Korea . . .

Somebody asked me what those fellows who fired Mac-Arthur were thinking about?

All I could say was they figure if we keep fighting this way . . . a man at a time . . . eventually the Chinese will get discouraged and quit.

Jody Maier said: "Seems like Japan tried that once."

There was the truth . . . clear as a fresh scooped cup of spring water.

Japan waged armed conflict with China for fourteen years. In the end it was Japan which, weakened, fell.

That is not what most of the fellows in Washington want for us. I am sure it is not. But they get tired and over-worked and the traitors in their midst keep giving them the needle . . .

It will be a couple of weeks before I see my hilltop in the Ozarks again.

I shall visit several cities in that time. Strange and wonderful cities.

Big places . . . big crowds . . . bright lights—where some men will pay half a week's wages to see a seventy-year-old French nightclub singer display her legs.

But I have seen the blue mist . . . where the earth and the sky have kissed, and the dancing white blossomed boughs of the hawthorn tree in the berry patch.

I have seen the stars at noon from the bottom of the barn cistern.

I know there is nothing wrong with us that could not be made right if we remembered who is the real leader of this nation.

He gave us everything we asked for . . . until we started thinking we could manage without Him.

Now when a nation's heart stops growing . . .

It better replant its feet in the sod.

Then and some sweat and some sunshine . . .

And maybe yet we can get back to God.

COMPETITION:

Old Homer McKee, the Hoosier Philosopher, used to say that Memorial Day affair in Indianapolis is not a car race. It is a test of the human race.

Out there on that track for five delirious hours half-a-hundred men will look death in the eyes, poke him in the ribs, slap him on the back, joust with him . . . jest with him.

What for?

Did you ever ride a hundred-plus miles an hour in an open race car no bigger than a bathtub with the sun parboiling your brain, wind flattening your face, ears splitting with the crash of cylinders? With the track and the world and your past pulling back under you like a torrent of hot milk —knowing maybe your whole future was just around the next turn up there where the blinding glimmer of a slick spot is rising up to slam you in the face?

And for what?

Men who would not sell their lives—gamble with them.

Those stakes are pretty high. Why?

Well, I'll tell you what Homer told me. He said that is the kind of Hades that hairy men come back to year after year just as they re-enlist in the Marines.

Because one of the lads out there has a new cotter pin he is testing.

He wants to know if it will hold.

Here is how he tells.

If he is alive when the race is over . . . it did.

Another lad has a new kind of steel steering knuckle he is going to test the same way.

What it takes to make automobiles safe those sweat-streaked track-monkeys are out to find out.

It is a question of their life . . . or yours.

These men are the guinea pigs who take the deadly germ of danger into their own blood and build up the anti-toxins that keep you and me and our children alive.

But they love it, you say . . .

I know.

So do the Marines.

That is what I mean.

The Soap Box Derby is that annual capitalist conspiracy designed to prove to 50,000 boys that only 141 of them can get to the finals and only one of them can win.

It's the biggest amateur racing event in the world.

The odds are even. The car must be made within specifications by the boy who drives it. Materials can cost no more than seven dollars and fifty cents and he has to prove it. All share the same unprejudiced power plant: the earth's gravity.

Jimmy, blond, grinning and fifteen, arrived from Columbus, Georgia, Tommy Jordan from Darlington, South Carolina, and Kurt Warncke from the American Zone of Germany, and Leroy West of Juneau, Alaska, and Darwin Cooper from Danville, Pennsylvania.

As each arrived . . . each of the 141 . . . he was met by Derby officials, and whisked through the streets behind a siren-shrieking police escort. They live at Derby town, their camp beside a lake where they meet other contestants and get their cars in top shape for the big race.

Then there is the trial run . . . the sleepless night before the big day . . . greasing the wheels until the bearings sing . . . up to the line . . . off down the hill . . . the ear-splitting crescendo of eighty-thousand screams and somebody wins.

The jet black number "34" with Jimmy, who works summers in a paint store in Columbus, Georgia, comes in fourth.

Then comes the strange paradox of Derby Day. Those eliminated from the early heats, who have lined the long ramp to watch later races, cheer the boys who beat them.

The final night there was a big banquet, and though only one had won . . . there were no tears . . . no long faces.

Instead, good-natured, back slapping also-rans talking enthusiastically about a new idea for sheering weight, steering or streamlining and saying "Wait'll next year!"

Wait until next year! A few years ago an ugly seed was planted in the sour soil of our depression. The seed grew into a weed sometimes called the "insecurity complex."

Whatever the botanical name, the seed was "suffering" and the weed was "fear."

It's an ugly, poisonous thing.

Fear of failure can cow strong men until they beg for the deliverance of some guaranteed mediocrity.

Underdeveloped adults, afraid to walk alone lest they fall, thinking the force of gravity is meant to drag them down, forgetting that without it we could not walk at all.

Since it was good politics, some played on this emotional weakness of our people.

The weed of fear flourished and spread and choked out the fragrant, but more fragile, flowers in our garden.

Parents disguised their fears with new cults and called themselves "progressive." In school, the lad was expected to learn without being taught.

At home, the only thing he learned at his mother's knee was how to dodge cigarette ashes.

So a generation grew up "hard" but not "tough" . . . "smart" but not "wise."

Today we have a new class of sophomores in our midst. Either they will take us back to the wide-eyed pride and chin-out dignity which was once ours, or we'll soon be walking on all-fours again.

It's going to take men with confident hearts and willing hands who know how to shape wood, wire the wheels, and work, and win or lose and try again, and they will have to be men who do not expect the ride down without the climb up.

Annually from Akron in Ohio's man-made Olympus, we are exporting to the corners of America the makings of such men.

Men unafraid to stand alone. Big enough to cheer the victory of another.

Men who know when somebody wins, somebody has to lose, that the race is never over and next time the loser may win . . . that there is a by-product of competition from which we all profit.

It makes even the last . . . fast. One outdistances the other, and all set the pace for the world.

Jimmy Gray from Tenth Street in Columbus, Georgia, won't be back next year. He tried three times before he

got as far as Akron. His next birthday will make him
ineligible.

But Jimmy took something home that is better than the
scholarship which went to the swiftest of them all—more
lasting than the automobile which was the prize for second
place—more important than the big awards which dollars
bought for the winners.

Jimmy will be a man now.

The kind we need so desperately.

He will not fear failure.

He has tasted the hot, dry acid of defeat in his throat. But
it was washed down with cake and ice cream and he knows
now it need not last.

For as long as he lives, the boy who came in fourth will
keep trying for first.

Knowing that what is really important is—not did you get
the prize—but did you try.

Not did you win the race—but did you feel the stinging,
singing, wonderful wind in your face.

What would Macy's be without Gimbel's? Minneapolis
without St. Paul? . . . and 1951 was Notre Dame's
greatest season.

From the time a boy learns to play marbles for keeps, he
improves his game. The freshman says "You bested me
this year, but wait'll next." As a sophomore he says, "You
did it again, but wait'll next year." And one day as a senior
it is his classmates who must congratulate him.

All have played better, worked harder, gone further . . .
competing.

I said 1951 was Notre Dame's greatest season. They were
tied once and they lost twice. They were shellacked by
those Southern Methodists and humiliated by Michigan
State. So they bounced back and beat the tar out of the
Trojans.

The real record is not on paper. It is etched on the hearts
of those lads who are no longer afraid to lose and who
know what it takes to win. It is a lesson books do not
teach.

It is not coincidence that Rome and Greece were greatest
when Romans and Greeks could throw the discus farthest.

It is no accident that Americans got the most of the juiciest
plums in the history of the world.

We reached for the high ones with one hand and planted
more trees with the other.

That's America: where we separate the men from the boys.

That is how since 1776 we have stretched our muscles,
and armor-plated our weaknesses, and put rivets in our
dreams.

THE RIGHT TO BE A BUM

I had meant to confine this just to generalities.

And embellish it with some fervent plea for the preserva-
tion of the Republic.

Then I got to thinking about a part-time dishwasher I know . . . who's a bum the rest of the time . . . and I tried to figure, what's his stake in all this free enterprise. How about the rag-picker . . . Or even that good-natured old janitor in the Northwestern train station . . . what's his percentage?

If he votes right and puts up a fight for freedom . . . what's his cut? "The government can't give you anything which it has not first taken away from you." He's heard that.

But he has nothing anybody can take away from him. So who's he to worry about whether the Constitution gets chopped up or the flag hauled down?

He's got nothing they can tax and nothing anybody'd want, so why shouldn't he take a bottle of cheap wine from the precinct committeeman and just vote the way the man says.

I had meant to talk about the American heritage . . . and I got to thinking about Joe the bootblack. What has he inherited? Well, I've been asking around. And the rest of you can tune out, now. And dial in three pages later. Because right now I aim to talk just to Joe the bootblack. And to Lennie, the part-time bum.

You know . . . I think that's what's wrong with the fervent flag wavers in this country. We spend too much time talking to one another.

But Joe and Lennie and Paul Harvey understand one another, too. Because they've all been flush and they've each been hungry and any one of them knows what it's like to work a hard seventeen-hour day for one dollar packing or sacking or stacking somebody else's groceries.

So we can speak the same language, and it's that language we're going to use here. The kind that'll be understood by Lennie and Joe and that vast mass of unorganized, unterrified human beings whose two-by-four house or third floor walkup is as close to the silk as they're ever going to get.

The rest of you just excuse us for a bit . . . if you will.

A while back a chap named Dean Russell made a speech out in Billings, Montana. Probably talking to a gathering of folks who already agreed with him.

I'm going to try to remember how he compared the American Negro slaves and the American Indians.

For a lot of years now we've been voting for the men who promise us government aid . . . of all kinds. We figured we wanted the government to guarantee to look after us.

Well, Sir, in the early American slave states . . . the law specified that the slaves must be taken care of.

The Constitution of the slave states generally specified that the slave owners must provide their slaves with adequate housing, food, medical care, and old-age benefits.

And the Mississippi Constitution contained this additional sentence: Quote: "The legislature shall have no power to pass laws for the emancipation of slaves . . . (except) where the slave shall have rendered the State some distinguished service."

Now get this . . .

The slave was guaranteed food, lodging, medical and old age care . . . but the *highest honor* the state of Mississippi could offer a man for distinguished service was to *set him free from this "security."*

The state's highest reward . . . was to give a man . . . the personal responsibility . . . of looking after his own welfare. Freedom to find his own job . . . or to be a bum if he liked.

Do you see why that's so important . . . just the right to be a bum?

And so the slaves eventually found freedom . . . to earn money they could keep . . . to build or buy their own houses; freedom to arrange for their own medical care and save for their own old age and THEN . . . *they weren't slaves any more.*

Let us on the other hand take the American Indians. These . . . we made wards of the government. These we gave "security."

We took away their freedom and gave them "security."

So they have become steadily less self-supporting.

I speak of the average, of course . . . not the spectacular exception.

In 1862 most American Negroes were slaves. Look at the remarkable progress in just one long lifetime later. Today the average American Negro is self-supporting, self-respecting, and responsible.

Today the average American Indian, it is said, will actually die of starvation unless he is fed by the government.

So we have to hire 12,000 federal employees to take care of 233,000 reservation Indians.

This has nothing to do with the color of a man's skin or the shape of his cheekbones. The Negro was free . . . to work or loaf; to starve . . . or to win a potful. The Indian was "secure." There was no reason for him to educate himself or learn to manage his own affairs or to be productive. It's not his fault; it's ours.

Just as it's going to be our fault . . . Joe and Lennie . . . our fault if we let them repeat this tragic error on us.

Simply because some arrogant would-be masters are convinced that today's Americans are too ignorant or too worthless to be trusted with their own destiny. They actually think that we would literally starve in the streets unless the government looked after our welfare. Welfare! Man, this is where we came in. They're on the way to buying and selling us again!

Now maybe you see what I started out to say.

You . . . You're a gandy dancer . . . You're a hod carrier . . . a trolley pilot . . . or you take tickets at the ball park . . . What have I got to lose, you say? Why shouldn't I take their offer of free medicine, money for work I don't do or crops I don't grow? Why not?

Here's why not, and don't ever forget this. "If your government is big enough to give you everything you want, it is big enough to take away from you everything you have."

And don't tell me you've nothing to lose. That's what they thought in Britain, too.

But already in Britain, elected leaders . . . can force the citizen to work wherever the government decrees they are most needed. Force!

In Russia, where this king of security got a slight head start, they'll make him work . . . if necessary . . . in leg irons.

You've nothing to lose, you say, because you're a bum?

That, Sir, is a priceless privilege . . .

In Russia you would be whipped or shot for it. It is your American right . . . to be a bum. That is part of being free.

So for Heaven's sake don't let them peddle this absurd "security" idea as something "new."

It was written into the Code of Hammurabi over four thousand years ago. The Romans called it "bread and circuses" to keep the crowd pacified while their sons died.

Karl Marx called it "socialism."

It's where the state makes laws "for your own good" whether you like them or not.

And Russia will imprison those who object.

It can't happen here?

Wait a minute, Mister . . . it has happened here.

Don't tell me you're still a hundred per cent free or I'll tell you about the owner of a small battery shop in Pennsylvania.

They told him he had to kick in money for his own social security. He didn't like the idea of being forced to buy insurance, and resisted.

The state confiscated his property.

Still he refused to obey.

So the state preferred criminal charges against him.

And in January of 1943 the government gave him the choice of conforming or going to prison. An enemy of the state . . . because he had refused to pay social security! He paid. His six months prison sentence was suspended.

From now on Lennie and Joe get this straight: you do have plenty to lose!

Whenever some of us try to warn you that big government wears brass knuckles . . . we're not trying to get you to fight for any other man's mansion.

We're trying to protect your equally important right to be a bum.

On election eve . . .

Listen and remember . . .

The guaranteed gifts . . . are just bait . . . nothing more. They'll offer the rewards of 1864 . . . A free meal, a free roof, a guaranteed job . . . and then . . . We're trapped into being somebody's slaves again.

And now recess—

PAGE THREE

Our immorality and political adolescence get a lot of advertising abroad. But most Americans are ashamed of the hussies, hoods, and heels that make the headlines.

Foreigners have heard our cannon; they missed hearing our church bells.

They judge the thickness of the callouses on our national conscience by Hollywood's fallen stars.

Actually we feel warmest inside talking about the ten thousand Sue Carroll and Alan Ladds living happily ever after.

We get a real boot out of watching Ben Hogan and Bobby Feller bounce back, even if they are not on our team.

And we go soft about a song called America the Beautiful because it calls by name the corners of this chunk of real estate we love.

We ourselves misjudge and misunderstand our nation; we incorrectly judge it by the headlines.

The "pulse" of the news is on page three. "Page three" is speaking figuratively of those happenings which do not measure up to page one news . . . and the "pulse" is just something you "feel."

Turn to page three. Turn away from the black headlines of page one . . . where the news is.

Turn to page three . . . where you can touch the pulse of the people.

Page one is a lie.

Page one never tells you when a man kisses his wife . . . only when he strangles her.

Page one is proof of nothing . . . except that one gunshot makes more noise than a thousand prayers.

Page three is where you meet the fine, friendly, God-fearing folks on Main Street . . .

They never do anything spectacular. They just love one
woman devotedly and perform one job well and one day
leave the world a little better for their having passed
through.

That is where the enemies of the United States underrate
us.

They read page one, which reports the doings of a handful
of exceptions.

Page three will let you see behind the lilac shaded windows into a hundred million private lives.

Let me show you what I mean . . . This is a story from
page three . . . especially for anybody who ever was a
boy . . . or anyone . . . who ever loved one.

The auction sale was on Main Street in Gibson City,
Illinois.

The community sale was progressing noisily . . . when
a small lad about eight . . . searching the merchandise
to be sold . . . came upon three baskets of small puppies.

As he looked over the puppies which someone had brought
to town to be sold, he came across the "special one." A fat
little fellow with his tail attached to his heart and both
going lickety-split.

Nobody else could have told what it was that set this one
apart from the rest . . . but the boy knew. He picked it
up and held the trembling few ounces of dog gently but
close.

It was ten-thirty in the morning when the boy first picked up the pup. They were still together at three.

By the time the auctioneer had come down the line and the pair of tractor chains had been sold . . . and the rug and washing machine, the first of the baskets of puppies was offered for sale.

Ten cents, twenty cents, do I hear twenty-five? . . . Twenty-five, do I hear thirty? . . . Sold for twenty-five cents.

The second basket "Twenty . . . twenty-five . . . thirty . . . sold for thirty cents."

When the auctioneer's helper reached down and removed the last pup from the lad's arms, somebody said twenty . . . somebody said fifty cents. Apparently someone else could see there was something special about this one.

"A dollar," one bidder said.

"A dollar fifty," shouted another.

"A dollar seventy-five!" And, "Sold for a dollar seventy-five to the lady in the bright red coat."

And the little lad took one last look—bit down hard on his lip . . . pulled his cap down to hide his eyes . . . and turned away.

He was across the Gibson City Main Street before the big wet tears began dropping from under his cap.

Then suddenly there was some confusion in the crowd behind him . . .

The auctioneer tried to sell a "like-new" umbrella stand
. . . when the red coat fought its way through the crowd
. . . following the boy.

With an attempt to overlook his tears and appear unmoved
she said: "Here, kid," and thrust the puppy into his arms.

And the sun came out on Main Street . . .
You couldn't see it . . .
But you could feel it.

Finally the auctioneer regained the attention of the crowd
and got a starting bid on the "like-new" umbrella stand.

I have not named the lady in the red coat, though I guess
everybody in Gibson City knows her name.

To single her out would not be fair to the many others who
ran the bidding up . . . So this pup sold for many times
the price of the rest.

You see . . . so many folks had the same idea.

CHAPTER IV

Seeds of Destruction

FATAL ERROR

In a careless moment a few years ago, we Americans gave away all our rights to property.

We abandoned the rights to private property for which our fathers fought with an innocent sounding constitutional amendment which reads:

> "The Congress shall have the power to lay and collect taxes on incomes from whatever source derived . . ."

According to this amendment, the government could take one hundred per cent. Today, on all income over eighty thousand dollars a year, the tax is 94½ per cent. So the end is in sight.

Already things are so bad tax-wise that the only way a good girl can get a mink coat is to steal it.

From history we know that the ultimate end of extravagance is bankruptcy.

Many years ago it was stated it would appear that success is to be punished; that exorbitant taxes have made it a crime for a man to prosper. The end result of such an order can only be the removal of incentive, the discouragement of our people, and the destruction of our free society.

These words were written by a man named Isocrates . . . ghost writer for the King of Persia . . . four hundred years before Christ.

And he was right. The golden age of Isocrates did end . . . in his own time.

This is a dead-end road we are on. Somewhere back there we turned left when we should have gone straight ahead.

Some political party had better get us back on the track.

We have too many Republicans shouting "hallelujahs" for Lincoln, yet refusing to heed his advice: "It is best for all to leave each man free to acquire property as fast as he can. Property is the fruit of labor. I do not believe in a law to prevent a man from getting rich."

Nor do contemporary Democrats have any right to claim Jefferson, yet ignore his warning: "We must not let our leaders load us with perpetual debt, and in its train . . . wretchedness and oppression."

Our national debt amounts to seven-thousand dollars for every family in America. And it is mounting every time the clock ticks.

Still we cannot pay our bills, win our wars, or keep our priceless heritage of individual dignity and liberty from slipping away.

There is no more soaking the rich; they have already had it. If the government took everything away from every man making 25 thousand dollars a year or more— take every cent he earns—all their money combined would not run the government for three weeks.

When there is talk about higher taxes, it is not talk about the rich any more.

The talk is about you and me.

The question is not whether the rich shall become poor, but whether the poor shall become slaves.

Those who would die to protect their precious freedom from a despot . . . are losing it in small bites—without a fight.

This Administration, or any administration, is going to find it too easy to spend and buy votes and too hard to curtail spending.

There will have to be a constitutional limit. Presently proposed increases would put taxes back at their World War II top level.

But if a few more states will take legislative action to request a Constitutional Convention we may yet insure a man's right to own property.

This movement on the part of the states is the voice of the people . . . this is grass roots.

Rarely before has there been a petition for a Constitutional Convention which has sprung up directly from the states.

Usually Congress asks them to ratify. This time the state legislatures are telling Congress what to do!

But taxes will not be cut as long as we have no constitutional protection from another squeeze . . . and another . . . and another.

Woodrow Wilson said, "The history of *liberty* is the history of *limitations* on the power of government."

I am convinced our only hope for limiting our malignant expansion of bureaucracy is to starve it—by cutting off the supply of tax dollars on which it feeds.

One day government is going to have to come to realize, as any housewife knows, that there simply are some services we cannot afford. There are some things we would like to have which just are not worth going bankrupt for.

But when Edward Nourse tried to sell this simple truth to the President, the President got himself a new economics advisor.

Yet you cannot exactly blame the President or the Congress—

How is anybody on Capitol Hill going to lop off any of these services when so many pressure groups have pet little projects which they just cannot or will not do without?

We all have our own private little row to hoe and nobody wants to trim his sails; yet if we do not we are not going to weather the storm that is brewing.

There is no such thing as controlled inflation. Historically, practically, there is no such thing.

Either we are going to have a rebirth of individual initiative in this country or we had better cash in our chips now because they will not be worth much after a few more "deals."

The farmer wants the government to economize on everything except price supports.

The Union League wants more economy in everything except government contracts for manufactured goods.

The Union Local wants more economy in everything except pensions and job insurance.

We are going to have to stand up and be counted on election day and say to the elected leaders . . . now get yourself up to Washington and stop playing ball and get down to business. Run this government like a business!

If a Senator or a Congressman keeps running the government deeper and deeper into debt we are going to have to bury him under such an avalanche of ballots he will never get out.

I have asked candidates from both parties: "Why don't you dare tell your constitutents that there are limits to what sound government can afford? Why don't you tell them we either get off this ice-cream diet or we are going to wake up one morning with the worst economic bellyache in the history of the world? Why don't you tell them?"

Some candidates said, "It is easy for you to talk but I have to get elected before I can do our country or anybody any good and I need votes to get elected; and let's face it, nobody wants to murder Santa Claus."

I don't want to murder Santa Claus. But on election day I am going to punch him in the nose if he doesn't get his hand out of my pocket!

Over two million Americans are now working for the Federal Government. That means, counting state and local government workers, that one out of every nine Americans already is working for the government.

If this trend continues it will not make any difference by what name we call our super state. Individual freedom will be gone. From then on the government can make us work any place at any job and at any wage or for nothing.

We should remember—no one came to this country originally or since—to found a government.

We came here to get away from government!

The same men who are selling us out with a lot of nonsense in the name of charity are the same men who are selling themselves for mink coats, deep freezers, and kickbacks on contracts.

A peg-legged con-man selling space in the Pentagon was caught.

But what about the legalized fleecing of taxpayers that goes on every day on Capitol Hill? What about the ten-per-centers who did business inside the White House, and planted a new deep freezer in the President's personal kitchen?

We have apprehended a one-time bootblack who conducted a friendship racket on the private telephone of the President's military aide.

But what about the countless cases of men in a position to throw government contracts to friends for a kickback under the table?

There is a class of crooks which has known its way around Capitol Hill for a long time. There was favoritism for a price under the Post Civil War administration of Ulysses Grant, but we just have not raised such a bumper crop of corruption before.

In recent years, it would appear we have come to accept as the norm—government by trickery, bribery, threat, intimidation, coercion, and murder itself.

Should we have a code of ethics for government officials? Some sincere individuals and others with a gift for espousing that which is popular say we should.

They say we should print a little book full of rules. Whenever a government official is about to make a compromise with his conscience he should refer to the index and see if it is permissable to take a kickback for granting a government loan.

It will not work!

If we are dealing with a man who does not instinctively know the difference between right and wrong, he is not going to bother to look it up in a book. If that were his desire, we already have such a book.

It has never been necessary to alter, add to, or otherwise amend the Ten Commandments. The book is there and any crook who wants to know what it says can steal the Gideon from his hotel room and find out.

We have the book but there is dust on it. The rules are plain, but there are too many of us trying to beat the game by making our own rules.

I have stood in the lengthening shadow of the Washington Monument and wondered how any man in the presence of such dignity could ever be mean or small.

I have looked up the Mall from the Lincoln Memorial to that stately marble monument to constitutional liberty on the hill and choked on a big chunk of fear. Not that anybody's bombs would ever destroy this white shrine to freedom, but that within its walls men, either too weak or too small, would lay down their load and go off to a cocktail party.

I know well from what has gone before, if all this stands for dies, it will not rise again. Daniel Webster said, "that which has happened but once in six thousand years cannot be expected to happen twice."

This magnificent accident, government under God, will not happen twice.

It is because I cherish it so that I say "no," a new rule book is not the answer. We cannot legislate honor among men. We will keep on reaping the bountiful harvests of freedom *if* . . . we deserve them.

Or we will lay aside the hoe, and let the harvest die and the weeds grow.

And one day the trumpet is going to blow, and we shall shout Halleujah! . . . which way to Paradise?

And the soft, calm voice of Final Authority will say, "You have had it, mister; you have had it."

MESS OF POTTAGE

Of all the inhabitants of the earth, man alone is capable of subjective reasoning. With this single advantage he has put all the rest of them in the zoo.

Recently I was told how man outwits his nearest mental competitor, the monkey. He ties a small-neck bottle to a tree. Puts bait in the bottle. The monkey can reach in, but with the bait clutched in his grip he cannot get his fist out again.

And he will not let go. So he is stuck, trapped by his stubborn greed.

Every election year in the United States the politicians are catching a lot of monkeys.

We have been baited with promises, pseudo prosperity and stage money. We have been lured into a trap.

In the past two decades in the United States . . . a beneficent government has sold us a substitute for freedom. It is called security.

At the polls—the people thought that was what they wanted—security.

Suddenly the gamble was taken out of job-seeking.

Taxes took all the excess profits—the bonus of business.

We were promised that the government will take care of us if we get ill or get old and that we shall never earn less than forty cents an hour no matter what.

Thus we have lost the good sense and moral integrity that set man apart.

We have decided, through some twisted reasoning, that crime is not wrong until we are caught. From the junior executive who chases the stenographer around the water cooler to the senior executive who subverts the tax collector, we are all trying to get something for nothing.

Honest self-sacrificing loyalty and sincerity of purpose have become so rare in our midst that we lionize the gallant sea captain who stays with his ship.

A generation ago we should hardly have expected him to do otherwise.

Today we have become so morally bankrupt that we are awed by such devotion to duty.

The fact that we are so much thrilled shows how far we have backslid.

If the old pioneering fire has died out of us, if we will hang onto new deals, fair deals and raw deals at the sacrifice of our I-deals, then we deserve to be trapped by our own clutching fingers because we are animals, nothing more.

History, for six-thousand years, is the record of free people made slaves trying to get the free lunch out of the bottle.

Lincoln said, "Let not him who is houseless pull down the house of another, but let him work diligently and build one for himself."

The Tenth Commandment God gave Moses at the top of Mount Sinai was to the effect that "thou shalt not covet anything that is thy neighbor's."

Somewhere up there in the silence, this great experiment
is watched; testing whether the immortal soul of man can
survive the carnal temptation to abandon, with increasing
incidence, our wives, our principles and this government
of free men under God which is the last good hope of
earth.

Shout "no" every election year! We will not have the
politicians of any party suggesting we alter or abandon the
Republic. Too long we have answered the noisy attack
with silence.

Shout "no!" Tell them that we are fed up with government
stealing from Peter to buy Paul's vote.

The uncertainty we feel is not the product of any storm
at sea . . . just the result of cunning, purposeful men
rocking the boat.

Tell them it is no deal!

We will not swap the feeling of being a king in overalls
. . . for the free feed we would get in the zoo.

What do they think we are . . . monkeys?

THE HOME-FRONT

In the United States we are plowing under, diluting, or
throwing away the very things our men in Korea are trying to buy with their lives.

Who is going to tell the frostbitten GI in the blasted
bunker why we let freedom evaporate? Who is going to
think up some shabby excuse for the kids who crawl like
ants up the stinking sides of a ditch full of dead men?

Why his dreams had to get shot full of holes? Why he had to spill his insides across some crummy, worthless Korean hillside, when the freedoms back home for which he thought he fought were stolen while he was away?

Our sons march to their graves thinking communism is their enemy when a super-state is moving in, unopposed, on the folks back home.

Uncle Sam is taking a terrific beating. He has lasted this long only because the old boy happens to have a remarkable Constitution.

Everywhere I hear sufficient concern for what is happening in Korea. Yet few seem aware—or seem to care—that while we are saying "no" to communism in Korea, we are buying the same tainted product for home consumption under another name.

Here it is called "planned economy." But it is still the super-state and it's offered, not as a temporary wartime expedient, but as a permanent substitute for freedom.

We submit to it and yet go on pretending that we are really opposed to communism!

We are the guardians of this Republic. It is we who have let fall the torch. We have been letting all our steam blow off in the whistle.

And the boys keep on marching.

It is an unfortunate fact that we seldom become aroused about the gradual loss of an intangible. Take the rug out of our parlor or five acres of our farm and we object violently. But steal some priceless unseen thing and we will barely notice and even more rarely object.

We have in this generation claimed that we have been fighting communism, which is nothing more or less than super-statism where the government decides what the individual deserves.

Yet, if every communist in the world dropped dead at ten-fifteen tomorrow morning we'd hardly miss them. We would still have the basic opposition of those who seek with varied weapons to destroy our Republic.

We have pretty well identified our two-faced friends who might destroy our Republic.

It is they who sneak distortions into the books and magazines we read, the movies we see, and the radio and television programs that invade our parlor.

Their weapons are sly innuendo, casual disrespect, printed mud and verbal garbage and always the glad hand for the educator they call "liberal" because he refuses to salute the flag, or the politician they praise for world-mindedness because he can make a Fourth of July speech without once mentioning any of the things we fought that war for.

Abraham Lincoln has said, "If this nation is ever destroyed, it will be from within, not from without."

Heiden, writing of the rise of Hitler, said, "There was no sudden general flocking to National Socialism, but rather a cynical lack of resistance to it."

Soviet Russia's objective is to prod us into national suicide . . . to keep us lashing our economic system into a gallop until it collapses around our ears.

For one thousand years, England was impregnable. Napoleon and Hitler could not storm across the Channel with all their bombs and guns.

But Karl Marx made it without firing a shot.

I personally would rather see my nation die, valiantly and cleanly under the H-bomb, than rot away under any cancerous form of any Godless slave-statism.

We are making it easy for Stalin.

If Stalin just keeps shouting "Boo!" ever so often . . . we will raise a bumper crop of economic ulcers over here and make it easy for him.

For two decades, now, we have been winning our wars. and losing our liberties—one "peace" at a time.

We have drugged ourselves with paper dollars. They are a narcotic, and we know it.

They make us feel strong—even as they weaken us. They are the drug that dulls the pain of reality while the effects last.

Unless we quit the habit in time and go back to work history will have to say we wasted away—on dope.

Only early cancer can be cured.

Our body economic has cancer. But we have not noticed because a phony prosperity is acting like a drug which temporarily relieves the pain while the body is eaten away.

We Americans, yet free to that degree, would not approve a Communist for public office.

We are, in fact, fighting and dying rather than submitting to this Godless alien ideology.

But are we consuming the same deadly poison under a different label?

We in the United States are now following a ten point program which was written in 1848 by a man named Marx and a man named Engels as a manifesto for the Communist Party.

This remarkable document constitutes the Ten Commandments for a true Communist. Here are its ten points of Communist doctrine for economic revolution:

(1) Expropriation of landed property and the use of land rents to defray state expenditure.

(2) A vigorously graduated income tax.

(3) Abolition of the right of inheritance.

(4) Confiscation of property of all emigrees and rebels.

(5) Centralization of credit in the hands of the state by means of a national bank with state capital and an exclusive monopoly.

(6) Centralization of the means of transport in the hands of the state.

(7) Increase of national factories and means of production, cultivation of uncultivated land, and improvement of cultivated land in accordance with a general plan.

(8) Universal and equal obligation to work; organization of industrial armies, especially for agriculture.

(9) Agriculture and urban industry to work hand in hand, in such a way as by degrees to obliterate the distinction between town and country.

(10) Public and free education for children. Abolition of factory work for children in its present form. Education and material production to be combined.

Not all the points are all bad. The good ones are the sleepers designed to make the rest sound innocent too.

The pattern is revolution.

Yet we, most of us unknowingly, have been following the pattern.

Of the ten points which Marx and Engels outlined in 1848 for economic revolution the United States in the past twenty years has adopted and put into practice six of them.

The adoption of the other four has, in some degree, been recently publicly recommended.

ONCE UPON A TIME

Once upon a time there was a great, powerful and good nation.

She was suffering from the aftermath of a war—from a depression.

Then came upon the scene a leader, an idealist, self-confident, intolerant of criticism.

Wisely he limited his early activities to combating the financial depression.

But in a while he regulated business, established new rules to govern commerce and finance, dismissed from his government such men as did not approve the new ideas.

The new leader saw that under the old system of free enterprise, landlords prospered. So he levied new taxes to take away their profits and destroy what he called "the monopoly of capital."

To please the laborers, he controlled prices.

To win the favor of the farmers he gave them loans and subsidies.

The national debt mounted alarmingly.

But the leader scorned his critics, saying that earlier leaders had not understood government finance.

Well, what do you say . . . did he build on rock . . . or on sand?

I say sand.

This is the story of Su Tungpo. The nation he led to its doom, a thousand years ago, was China.

It was internal decay rather than external attack that destroyed the Roman Empire.

Starting about 146 B.C. internal conditions in Rome were characterized by a welter of class wars and conflicts. Street brawls, corrupt governors, lack of personal integrity and moral responsibility demanded reform.

About 290 years after Christ a Roman Emperor named Diocletian took over. He really grabbed the bull by the horns. He took over in a period of turmoil and severe depression.

The first thing Diocletian did was close the banks and call in the gold and start a broad program of reform.

He reduced the power of the Senate and delegated that power to government bureaus.

He also raised taxes and put millions of people on the public payroll.

But when this failed to do the job . . . the country was still in trouble . . . he asked more personal powers for himself. For a brief while they were standby powers.

Then he used them. All at once he froze wages, he froze prices, he froze jobs and he stopped profits. He dictated to the farmer what he should plant and when and how much he should sell it for—and he rationed food.

What happened? The labor market closed down—incentive was gone.

Farm life became dependent on bureaucratic red tape and exorbitant taxes cost the farmer his land. He kept for himself only enough to grow turnips for his family and lost the rest to the state.

Without food and with incentive gone, city life stagnated and Rome passed into what history has recorded as "The Dark Ages," lasting a thousand years.

Rome fell apart because *within* it had decayed and degenerated morally, socially, and economically to where, like an angry scorpion, it turned on itself and died of its own sting.

What happened to Rome and Spain and Greece and China
. . . *decay from within* . . . can happen now to the
United States.

THE DEATH RATTLE

There is a hideous sound just before death comes. Most
soldiers and all doctors know the sound. It is not the
agonizing scream that tears the air, not the sobbing of a
last despair, but after that, the rasping, ugly rattle of
death.

Empires, too, make such a sound before they fold their
wings—any historian recognizes it.

It is not the excited staccato of gunfire in the streets, no
great bombs shattering the sunset calm, no single, sharp
outcry signals when a nation is about to die. It is a more
frightful sound than that.

It is a human cackle coming from dim-lit windows above
the silent streets, a calloused laugh from one who steals,
but rarely buys.

It is not the verbose, violent protest of the anarchist in
Pershing Square which says the end is near.

It is not when citizens object, or correct, or reject. Men
can flail their government with the ten-tailed lash of anger
and make it stronger.

It is when they laugh, that the end is near. When a government is mocked by the snide snickers of its own citizens,
that is the death rattle with which empires die.

I recently heard such a sound from the lips of a silly girl.
I heard freedom begin to gasp its last. A stenographer, in

a city crying for stenographers, has chosen instead to spend the summer at the holiday home of her parents in the Indiana dunes—collecting unemployment compensation.

There have always been parasites among our people. Some of those who originally populated America's West panhandled their way or dodged work with a deck of cards.

But it was our present generation which was the first ever to make robbery respectable. Being a loafer is no longer a misfortune; it is a profession.

I have seen a recent Nielsen survey of the rather typical American town of Aurora, Illinois. One out of every five persons on relief there was ineligible.

Some refused to work, some did not even live in the state but at resorts outside the state; yet we were paying them to loaf out of our already stifling tax burden.

Get a survey in your own community!

See how many you find like two persons in Chicago who were taking ten-thousand dollars in relief funds over the past eight years although one of them was employed all the while. Incidentally, they came to this country from Mexico more than twenty years ago and have not yet applied for citizenship.

In Illinois a man can arbitrarily refuse a job and still collect unemployment compensation.

Jacob Panken, justice of Domestic Relations Court in New York City, says, "Relief is ruining families."

Judge Panken is a lifelong socialist. He said that out of eight million persons in New York, one hundred and sixty-seven thousand were on relief.

Every day he sits in court he amasses new evidence that the relief setup is sapping their will to work—encouraging paid vacations at public expense.

He says it is possible to shed all self-respect, refuse all jobs offered, buy all the liquor you want, desert your wife and live with somebody else, and the welfare department will provide you with an income of $3,680 a year tax free.

I talked to a newspaper official who had been surveying the want ad situation. According to him one class of employee is making a business of living off the government, working a few weeks and drawing unemployment pay for months.

When the college graduate stenographer announced she was spending the summer on the dole in the Dunes, I realized how twisted our thinking has become.

Ponzi, the famous swindler, collected from investors and used part of the payment from each new investor to pay interest to a previous one . . . until they caught up with him.

Government handouts are like that—a glorified chain letter.

They are a fake and somebody has got to get stuck with the bill.

The price we shall have to pay will be the liberty we once loved so much that generations of Americans offered to die to preserve it.

Let us not foolishly assume that we are subsidizing our lazy job dodgers to keep them from becoming communists.

If poverty and hardship were the causes of communism, our suffering and underprivileged Forefathers would have become communists instead of Americans.

They had their bellies full of the so-called government "security" of Europe. They were willing to leave their homes and their land, to risk privation, disease, death and torture by savages—to be free of it.

The communism which is corrupting Americans today is not a movement inspired by the poor, but by the cowardly pseudo-intellectual rich. The Paul Robesons, the Frederick Vanderbilt Fields, and the Alger Hisses suffer from the guilt complex of those to whom success came too cheaply.

Some college students and some of their professors not long enough away from their mothers seek to substitute a big, beneficent government as a guarantor of their security.

Communism is not born of empty stomachs, but of immature intellectuals who want to be wet-nursed all their lives.

Karl Marx founded communism. He was a failure in school who could not get along with his own family.

Karl Marx did not want for money. He was befriended and subsidized by a capitalist, Friedrich Engels, so that he could destroy capitalism.

Today all of Soviet Russia suffers from that same sense of inferiority and seeks to wreck the obviously superior government of the United States.

While we are subsidizing the lazy job dodgers, those of us who work assume tax burdens which will bankrupt the nation.

Twenty of the last twenty-two years our government has been spending beyond its income. This year our government is going to collect sixty billion dollars. But our government will spend a hundred billion!

In 1932 President Franklin Roosevelt said, "For three years I have been going up and down this country preaching that government—Federal, State, and Local—costs too much. I will not stop this preaching."

They have not stopped preaching.

But they have not stopped spending either.

With just our Federal Government hiring new civilian workers at a rate of a thousand a day, it is important to remember that the toughest balloon will take just so much hot air.

If we do not stop blowing we are going to awaken one morning and find we are all working for the government, that the government now owns the house, the car, and the mortgage on the church.

A revolution by evolution, without Stalin firing a shot.

CHAPTER V

Korea

THIS IS WAR

We are told that what is happening in Korea is not really a war.

But a lot of American boys are just as dead as if it were.

I am going to call it what it is: a bloody, rotten, thankless war.

They have told the boys in Korea just to keep dying quietly and not to ask questions.

They have discouraged honest reporting of this thing, deleting by censor those front-line dispatches which described too graphically what it is like in the line.

I don't intend just to remind the boys what it is like. They know.

They can't say what I am going to . . . Korea is a war.

Whatever it says on the tombstones at Arlington, those men died hard. With the taste of their own hot blood in their throats, they cried when they died and it hurt when they did.

They died not just once. Every night in the clammy sack they fingered the snapshot from home and didn't cry, and wondered why.

There is a brisk snap in the wind off the rice fields tonight. It will be winter again soon.

The Pentagon is advertising its efforts to get the lads who have been used most home first.

Yet what is really happening tonight is that veterans of the very first days of the Korean War . . . are moving up for more. Corporal Jack Hacker of Bloomington, Illinois, was shot up by a burp gun at Taejon in August of 1950. He is back in the line tonight, somewhere north of Seoul. He didn't want to go back. Pfc. Garland Couch of Union Grove, Alabama . . . Sgt. Jim Bordelon of New Orleans . . . Lads of the 34th . . . the second American regiment to arrive in Korea, more than a year ago. These are old-timers.

A little while in Japan has not erased the memory of what it is like to feel your feet freezing in your own sweat.

At home the headlines are all about truce talks, because a truce that is a dream is easier for the home folks to sleep on than a war that is a nightmare.

"American Infantry Takes Tallest Peak in Heartbreak Ridge." That is the kind of headline we like . . . with all the dirt washed off.

The censor won't allow identification of the famous in-fantry outfit that clawed its way up that blood-slick hill-side and routed the filthy, fanatical, frightened little savages from their holes one mortar, one grenade, one knife blade at a time.

I don't pretend to know the answers.

But I do know some of the questions of the boys and maybe if we can drag their fight out from under wraps and call it by its right name—maybe if folks can see it better—wiser ones than myself—we will be able to figure out what to do about it.

To some, Korea is a football.

Apparently to others the blood of the boys is intended to cleanse them of the responsibility for the ten years they have been playing footsie with those killers out there in the dark.

To some, Korea is an excuse for more and more centralization of authority. The Pied Pipers use somebody else's gun . . . to back us into their trap.

Maybe to a few, Korea is what they say it is. A challenge intended to stop Soviet Russia.

Maybe they really believe we have got to contain communism where it is, or be consumed by it. If they do, if this is their studied view, then I say it is high time they carry out the plan and get it over with.

When the cost of the Korean War is added up here is something to remember.

In three years of bloody battle with Japs, jungle rot and assorted diseases, in three years of World War II in the southwest Pacific under General Douglas MacArthur, we lost twenty thousand American lives.

So far in this war, fighting with weapons and tactics prescribed by the United Nations, that many American soldiers have died in half that time!

I am not speaking for the "big brains" in Washington now. They have their say every day.

I am speaking for the lad in the line, who has not tasted hot food or felt a dry bed in a month and who has not washed under his arms in three.

I am speaking for the lad who is crawling up some nameless Korean hillside on his belly, without purpose, plan, or objective.

Times when there's been something very right, but very hard to do, I have found my own inertness overcome by a combination of conscience, conviction, and a good kick in the pants to get me started in the right direction. So maybe this will help.

It is a brief note scribbled in pencil from somewhere north of Chorwon.

I will read you all but the personal part . . . and not the signature. Things are rough enough on the lad without this backfiring:

"September 29th. We walked up the hill without opposition. Since then we have had fourteen killed in action, twenty-eight wounded in action, and four missing in action.

Last night the company was surrounded and attacked by the North Koreans. The company kept drawing up toward the top of the hill and the 'Gooks' were all around. It was

the most awful thing I have ever known. Three men blew
their tops when dawn broke.

They captured a Sergeant (during the night) and tortured
him to death, making him call for help until the guys on
the hill couldn't stand it. He screamed for three hours,
and they moved him closer and closer but our men weren't
able to get him. He was blinded and mutilated when . . ."

I said I would read it all. But I will not. What I am trying to say is that it is no Sunday school picnic in Korea
. . . there's a war on.

It is not always clear whether our dog faces and our diplomats are fighting for the same things. What is important is,
we are asking our sons to go through that to "preserve, protect, and defend" us.

Past a point, patience is no longer a virtue. Impatience
with the old world led us to the new one.

It was our impatience that stopped Hitler at the Channel
instead of the Hudson.

There is a time to lose your patience and use your temper.
There came a day when Jesus' last recourse was to stride
into the corrupt temple with a piece of twisted rope in his
clenched fist and smash up the furniture.

A familiar quotation was paraphrased this way by Congressman Bender of Ohio: "If you keep your head when
all about you are losing theirs . . . maybe you just don't
understand the situation."

Maybe we just don't "understand the situation."

A hundred thousand American boys have been shot up in this gunfight. Yet we can't even find it in our hearts to write a song about Korea.

Never has a war been so utterly lacking in inspiration that it stumped the modern music mercenaries. But this one has. So there will be no songs about Korea.

Men will just keep marching to the sound of little tin horns, soaking up three thousand pints of blood per month from home, and with outdated weapons and behind a mongrel flag they will just keep marching.

CHARLIE'S RETURN

Let me tell you about Charlie who died in Korea, and about the kind of questions he may have asked had he survived.

I have received a letter the essence of which is: Charlie came home last week . . . in a box, under a flag.

All of his friends were at the church. The pastor said some kind words, concluding "He died for freedom."

He knew Charlie well. Charlie was a shipping clerk. Graduated last year from high school, same class with his daughter. His children and the banker's children went to the same school with . . . the widow's son.

Charlie was too young to die. He had not seen twenty years, while the prophets give us three-score-and-ten. Charlie was cheated out of fifty years.

Hear the details of how he died. The Reds bombed an unprotected outpost. Why unprotected? Because Americans cannot defend themselves against raids from Manchurian bases. Those are the United Nations' rules.

Charlie came home in a box. He died for freedom.

What was Charlie doing in Korea? There is no war there, only a police action.

And who started this police action? Not New York; not California or Texas; not even the whole United States.

The United Nations sentenced Charlie to Korea, and set the rules under which he might fight.

The rules were written by felons like Hiss and fools in striped pants.

Felons and fools left Charlie "unprotected" and he came home in a box.

Charlie did not die seeking the Holy Grail of freedom like the Minute Men of Concord, or the Marines in Belleau Wood or the Seabees in the Gilberts or the foot soldiers on Guadalcanal.

Charlie was a martyr to the unholy ambition of those who would regiment the whole world under their infamous banner of International Free Love.

And Charlie came home in a box.

How long, O Lord, must mothers and widows weep? How long, O Lord, must sons and husbands claw their way to the crest of Heartbreak Ridge, there to become a human sacrifice to the pagan gods of war?

That is all it was. Make nothing more or less of it than this. He was a human sacrifice, and he came home in a box.

But Charlie, had he lived, may have had to answer the kind of question parents are often confronted with. There is no parent who has not sometime blushed at the naked crux of a child's blunt question. Wise parents try to keep even, with such homework texts as Spock and Lawler and the rest. But one day your son will say "Dad, what ever happened to white bread?"

You will have to know what to say . . . Maybe this will help.

Tell him that back in 1948, his government set out to help feed the rest of the world. A by-product of this program (called "Point Four") was to create an artificial prosperity in the United States during an election year.

It is rather like giving you laughing gas for an amputation.

They earmarked one and a quarter million dollars for India. But then in 1950, his government gave India ninety million dollars' worth of wheat. Then, in a secret agreement in 1952, his government, without asking, gave India another fifty million dollars.

There were similar election-eve handouts to other governments and this is what happened to white bread.

Your bread is black now, son, because . . . well, it is part soybeans and sawdust. We do not have so much wheat as we used to have.

What happened to coal? In 1951 we were sending coal to Europe . . . well . . . here . . . this will say it best: We loaded up a freight train with coal; the train was so long it stretched from New York to San Francisco and back again! Every car loaded with coal. We sent all of that to Europe in 1951. Of course, we never got it back and never got paid for it.

Son, you asked what happened to white bread . . . The Europeans who got coal free from us used their dollars to buy from other people. So our taxpayers had to pay our coal miners with dollars we had saved for South American beef. When we could not buy the beef we had to pasture our wheatland and that is what happened to white bread.

Coal was just a part of what we gave away.

Between 1942 and 1952—ten years—we loaded up a freight train with silver dollars. Every car in this great freight train was loaded to capacity with silver dollars. The train stretched from Dallas, Texas to Washington, D. C. We sent that to Europe, too.

The Europeans spent a lot of these dollars buying stuff from the United States, and all that commerce made us feel rich for a while. They used our money to buy machines made in Detroit by farmer boys from Ohio.

But when the balloon burst and the boys went back to Ohio their tractors were ten years old and all the newer ones had been sent away.

Taxes were so high the farmer could not afford help, so he was struggling just to feed himself. He had to squeeze the last drop of fertility out of his acres without putting any back, and when he lost his farm to the government for back taxes, it would not grow grain anymore.

That is what happened to your white bread!

You wanted the truth, son. I guess you mean the "whole" truth.

We did not send all your bread overseas.

We let our government buy votes from our own people with part of it. In 1951 we handed out eight billion, five hundred million dollars to civilian government employees. Not soldiers, son . . .

By 1952 there was only one tiny little county in the whole United States—Armstrong County, South Dakota—population, fifty-three—which was the only speck on the map of the United States where there was not at least one of these jobocrats living off the taxes of others.

With all these parasites having to eat food, when seventy per cent of them should have been growing it or processing it, we fast ran short of it.

That is what happened, son, to your white bread . . . and to ice cream and orange juice, too. That is what happened to beefsteak, son.

A ninety billion dollar federal budget ate it up.

A third of it to run your government, and two thirds of it to help other governments which were thus discouraged from helping themselves.

A wise statesman tried to warn us. He said a man can carry three hundred pounds across the room but not around the block without breaking his back. But we grabbed the three hundred pounds, posed vainly for the crowd, and started around the block.

That is how it is we are having black bread.

I am sorry, son. I would never have done this to you, son, but we thought it would last forever.

You have to believe me, son.

I did not mean to do this to you.

Hear me, please.

They told us we had to.

Son, come back here!

Son! . . . He's gone . . . I guess I didn't explain it very well.

He thinks it is my fault.

THE MACARTHUR INCIDENT

A real American statesman would say about this mess today: "The Russians are cynically confident that they will, in the end, inherit" . . . not fight for, but will inherit "the fruits of our civilization. Russians despise Americans."

It did not take a State Department expert to get this inside information. That was said by Teddy Roosevelt more that fifty years ago.

Then he added: "But I look upon the Russians as a people to whom we can give points and still beat them."

He was not afraid.

In essence, the orders the politicians gave to General Mac-
Arthur were these:

Do anything you want of a tactical military nature. But
do nothing which could have political implications.

For example, you may bomb the southern half of a Yalu
River bridge; that is a military matter. But not the north-
ern half; that is political.

You may drop little bombs on the enemy, but not big
bombs; that would be political.

You may use half of our Seventh Fleet to kill all the communists you can reach on both coasts of North Korea. But
you must use the other half of that same Seventh Fleet to
protect the communists on the China mainland from the
Formosa forces of Chiang Kai-shek.

This sounds like a comic-opera war . . . a Gilbert and
Sullivan gunfight. We could laugh if it were not all so
very tragic.

The Supreme Commander, being an honorable man,
obeyed his orders to the letter. He violated none of these
absurd prohibitions. He saw his gallant handful die . . .
when by other battle tactics they might have lived.
Yet he obeyed his orders.

Then one day he received a letter from a Congressman
which asked certain questions. He had been taught that
in a Republic it is entirely proper for citizens to communi-
cate their views to Congressmen.

But in this he erred.

Though his recommendations were purely military the Congressman happened to be a Republican. That made the matter political.

Therein did the great General sin.

He had been away from home so long that he did not realize how things have changed.

So they stripped him of his authority and told him to go some place . . . anyplace . . . just go.

Korea was left an open, bleeding wound. The man who sought to stop the bleeding at its source . . . was dismissed.

Like Rome and Greece and Spain and France and England before . . . we want to bleed to death.

What has happened to the General is not new. The military has received its orders through a waxed mustache before.

More than one hundred and fifty years ago, Britain's greatest Admiral, Lord Nelson, paced the quarterdeck of his warship off Copenhagen.

Danish resistance was unexpectedly savage. Constant din of cannon made talking almost prohibitive, but the men saw no fear in the face of their Captain and all was well. The Danes had thrown in more than he had counted on. Therefore three of Nelson's ships were aground and one afire.

Yet, there was no anxiety over the miscalculation. The man who was destined to end Napoleon's rule of the sea at Trafalgar brimmed with eagerness for the fray. The muscles of his face were tense with anticipation as he shouted his commands.

Suddenly a signal officer raced to the Admiral's side. Sir Hyde Parkar's flagship had hoisted the signal to break off the battle . . . to discontinue the action . . . to retreat.

"What!" Nelson demanded furiously. His perfumed, snuff-sniffing, lace cuffed superior was ordering him to turn and run!

Nelson raised his telescope, pressed it against his *blind* eye and said: "I see no such signal." He went on to win the fight.

General MacArthur wanted to call a war a war and fight and finish it. But he got the sack.

As a result of General MacArthur's words to Congress the American people came to be divided into two schools of thought.

General MacArthur says let us knock out our enemy and stop dying and get back to living.

The present policy is, it appears, to exhaust ourselves fighting preliminary bouts . . . thus leaving Stalin fresh to finish us off.

I leave it to the reader to say . . . which is the American way?

If being just "American" is no longer proper . . . then let us face the facts.

Let us realize that the logical progression of our present policy is to wage war only on their terms and buy peace only at their price.

Then, if all Stalin wants is territory, how long will it be before our State Department offers him Texas?

Since MacArthur was dismissed, truce talks have been undertaken with the enemy.

If they should fail, our "thinkers" will be doubly reluctant to start bombing Red bases in Manchuria and blockading the China mainland because this would amount to an open admission that MacArthur knew the score a long time before anybody else.

Therefore, truce must be bought at any price to establish a line across the most narrow waist of Korea and announce that, as far as we are concerned, the war is over. We would leave most of Korea in the hands of the South Koreans, only some worthless mountain acreage remaining in North Korea.

To some of us, however, it is inconceivable that the enemy, meaning now all communist interests in Asia, would sit still for such a split.

They would, instead, seek to scatter other United States forces . . . through other, similar, stalemate wars . . . until we, overextended, followed colonial Britain into bankruptcy and oblivion.

LET'S FINISH IT

A deadline must be set for the end of the present fruitless strategy in Korea . . . it must not be allowed to go on indefinitely.

I have paid my income taxes. I have contributed to the support of a lot of things which I would consider bad investments if I were making a freer choice.

But my tax dollars did buy for me one vote in this biggest of all corporations; as a stockholder in America I am entitled to one vote.

I vote that we make this phony war a real one and I recommend, on the basis of General MacArthur's proposal, that our first battle maneuver be to silence our little guns and stop killing Chinese and stop killing Americans and get out our big guns and get this thing over with.

I am fed up with the pussy-footing policy which permits our State Secretary to sun himself in Bermuda and the rest of us to pay more attention to stock dividends than to the Korean death count just because we are far enough away from the fight so we can't hear American boys cry before they die . . .

I am sick and tired of saving face for the State Department by a half-hearted holding action in Korea.

Tonight all "face-saving" means to the man in the foxhole is keeping his from getting shot off. In this case, I think, his perspective is better than ours.

The magnificent MacArthur obediently abided by the United Nations' Marquis of Queensbury rules while he shadow-boxed with assorted Orientals just to keep us from remembering that our own government officials supported the Communist cause in China for the past two decades.

If we let them nail the men of MacArthur to a cross for made-in-Washington mistakes and treasons, then our disgrace will be greater than defeat could possibly be.

Washington's political bigamists are eager to forget the Alger Hiss and kindred affairs by going through the motions of opposing communism.

But they still do not want to admit we are at war because, for one thing, that would mean fifty-five thousand catalogued Communists in our own country could be jailed by the FBI.

So the Korean war is called a police action in behalf of the United Nations.

Just loyal Americans get shot; the disloyal go free.

This way we can continue to allow the enemy's fifth column inside this country passkeys to our press and information facilities, to our defense plants, and to our vital labor unions.

We continue allowing Red reporters, who can spy on the side, to snoop around meetings of key committees in our nation's capital.

I speak for no political party and for no policy making group. I speak merely as one stockholder who has on his conscience the smashed-in face of a man who lies beneath the blood-crusted clay of No-Name Ridge . . . Just a bayonet sticks out of the half frozen earth to mark his final resting place.

He can't be heard now; his vote's gone; his stock in the United States was confiscated when he died. So somebody has to speak his piece.

What strength Soviet Russia has she is smart enough not to waste. Instead she prods the nations around her perimeter into wasteful wars with us, designed eventually to cut us down to her size.

China has bankrupted every invader for six thousand years. When we boastfully announce the enemy's casualty count, Stalin smiles.

He knows it costs the United States $108,000 to kill one enemy soldier; he knows a million Chinese die every year of starvation anyway.

To have to feed China could keep Soviet Russia broke and busy for two hundred years. Instead, Stalin goads them into war with us and we obligingly assist in solving Asia's biggest problem of over-population.

While our bombers desist from striking at China's weakest point, the sources of production, we spend men—our most scarce commodity—spinning our wheels in Korea's mud.

That is why I vote for war.

In behalf of the unnamed GI of No-Name Ridge . . . I say let us untie the hands of our military men and let us choose the weapons from now on.

That's "us" spelled U.S., not U.N.

Dr. Vannevar Bush said that right now we have it in our power to wipe out Soviet Russia's means of making war completely—if we used nothing more than just our atomic weapons. And atom bombs are now a fourth-rate weapon in America's arsenal for war.

If we have any dignity, decency, and sense of respect for that lad who died face-down in blood and mud, then let us stop killing more of our boys one bullet at a time.

Unless he is to have died for nothing, let us resolve that:

> Acknowledged and unrepentant Communists in this country should be jailed now and promptly deported to the land of their first allegiance.

> Communists in Korea should be held where they are, while we blockade China's Reds with every means available to the freedom-loving peoples of the earth.

> Bomb their industry!

> Bomb their lifelines of communication and supply! It required only two bombs of the right kind to discourage Japan. Paralyze China's commerce!

> Close their ports! Until she sees the error of her ways, stop anybody from trading with China.

If Soviet Russia wants war we might as well find it out while the best weapons are in our hands.

If Soviet Russia does not want war—and believe me she does not want the kind I am talking about—then we can stop this stupid killing and dying in places we can't pronounce, for territory we don't want.

We have got to find the courage to say "All right, Kremlin, either stop—either get your fists open and shake hands—or else come out into the middle of the ring fighting. But we are not going to waste any more of our strength getting down and wrestling with all your in-laws."

Soviet Russia cannot wage a full scale war.

Let us not wait until the best weapons are hers while the United States continues to be weakened from within by saboteurs, wasted resources and worthless money.

In one last salute to the lad of No-Name Ridge I vote we go to war in Korea.

If we send more and more Americans to follow him into the same trap, then he died for nothing.

But if from his sacrifice we learn the names and addresses of our real enemies . . . and the size and shape of our best weapons . . . then he may rest less restlessly.

There are those of our own people who seek to keep us in unofficial bayonet fights indefinitely.

They are looking out for Soviet Russia's best interests, not ours.

In behalf of a dead man, I protest.

What could possibly give more aid and comfort to the Kremlin than for us stupidly to continue to dissipate ourselves to death with a drunken orgy of spending for everything and swinging on everybody and hitting no one.

After Korea, a war we could win in sixty days if we really wanted to, there will be Yugoslavia, Indo-China, Formosa, Burma. And the list is endless.

The Kremlin will be merely calling signals; it will not carry the ball.

Russia will not fight us for any of these lands because Russia does not have the power, and we have.

Let us quit swinging short of the target. Let them know now that the next move in any direction and we klobber the Kremlin.

I vote we call a war a war and aim for a knockout before we get whipped on points.

The issue, succinctly stated, is this: Do we hold the enemy at bay with bombs . . . or do we continue to send more and more American boys marching off into the face of 300 million bayonets . . . one at a time?

The silent spirit of the unknown soldier of No-Name Ridge looks eastward out to sea . . . wondering what your vote will be.

CHAPTER VI

Insurance for Tomorrow

HOW IT IS DONE

If you want to give Junior a test to determine his manual dexterity, you never say "Come here, Junior, I'm going to give you a test."

Instead, you say, "Junior, let's you and I play games . . ." You take the square pegs and the round holes and the round pegs and the square holes and play games . . .

Very soon you have a quite accurate measure of Junior's manual dexterity.

On the international level, the Soviet Union enticed the United States into a game of military chess using Korean soldiers as pawns. In this manner the Russians obtained an accurate measure of our weapons and our dexterity at handling them.

When you want Junior to give you something . . . you never say "Here, Junior, give me that ball." Oh no! You would have a fight on your hands for certain.

Instead, you say, "Here, Junior, you give me that new ball and I will let you have this fine old ball."

On the international level, Soviet Russia says: "Here, little USA, we are going to let you play again with the trains, planes, and barges in Berlin but you give us China!"

Delightedly the little USA announces "Look, we broke the Berlin blockade!"

You never say "Junior, eat your spinach."

Instead you say, "Which would you prefer, Junior . . . spinach or carrots?"

For the sheer joy of self-importance in being allowed a choice, Junior says "Spinach."

Soviet Russia says . . . now little USA . . . which would you prefer to protect today . . . Korea or Tibet? Little USA says "Korea" and abandons Tibet . . . without protest.

It is not even advanced adult psychology they are using on us . . . it is elementary child psychology . . .

But they are making it stick. We're up to our collar buttons in spinach!

By using tricks employed in dealing with children they have kept us busy in Berlin while they stole China; they have kept us busy in Korea . . . while they have stolen Tibet.

Where will the Kremlin strike next?

Soviet Russia, with agents close to the British Foreign Office, knows that Britain will not fight for Iran's oil. Britain will bluff . . . but will not fight for Iran's oil.

So, Soviet Russia, with bad supply lines to that source . . . will end up with it, anyway. And will take care of the supply lines later.

So the cancer of communism spreads . . . feeding itself on the weakened wills of the world's hungry and afraid. And so it will continue to spread until we get our eyes open and our fingers out of our ears . . . and pinpoint the responsibility for aggression . . . at its source.

The communist timetable of conquest is flexible, but the pattern is plain.

Soviet Russia's avowed and published intention is to catch us with four million men armed, equipment built for eighteen million, and no war . . . thus completely to unbalance our economy, create depression, panic, chaos, and take over what's left with agents already planted inside our country.

Then as in the case of Czechoslovakia, Romania, Hungary and Bulgaria, Soviet Russia . . . here too . . . would achieve all she wants without fighting for it.

It should be remembered that no agreement with the Kremlin is possible.

Rudolph Menshinski, former Soviet Consul-General in Berlin, said:

"We should promise all that is asked and as much as one likes, as long as we can get something tangible in return . . . and as long as there are idiots to take our signatures seriously."

With that announced philosophy of doing business, Soviet Russia continues to swallow one nation after another . . .

and, all the while, continues to consume us . . . in small bites.

We cannot afford the endless effort required to rescue the world's two billion human beings one at a time.

We cannot take over foreign peoples and grow strong. History shows that to take over foreign peoples is to grow weak.

It is like eating too many green apples.

Two billion human beings who are not Americans and do not want to be are more than we can fight, feed or finance.

But we can make the gangsters leave them alone while they learn to feed themselves.

We can scare the pants off the Kremlin crowd if we let them know we know the score . . . and that if they get out of line once more . . .

We will not again try local first aid with footsoldiers . . .

Our bombers . . . will stop the bleeding . . . at its source.

Let us get smart. Let us grow up and use a little psychology of our own.

COMMONSENSE PRECAUTION

In flying, we lay the navigation map on the table and draw a straight line from here to there. Then, either with radio aids or by dead reckoning, seek to follow that line.

If, due to a miscalculation or a wind shift we drift off course, we correct it, gradually, until we are back on the beam. If we encounter ice or severe turbulence, we try to alter our course and go around it.

If we suddenly run up against a storm that is too dangerous to tackle and too big to by-pass, we turn around and make the trip another day.

Only a stubborn fool would do otherwise.

A man or a nation must be consistent about objectives.

We should know where we are going. But there are many times in the affairs of men and of nations when we should reconsider *how to get there.*

It has been some time since the great debate over countering communism. Recently former President Herbert Hoover said that it is time that we recalculate risks and reconsider alternatives. According to him we are "off course" and unless we correct our navigation quickly we are going to run out of gas—a long way from home.

A year ago we were told that there would be a European army of more than forty divisions by the end of 1952, with twenty more by the end of fifty-four.

What's happened?

The French, who had promised fifteen divisions by the end of fifty-two, now say that they meant only ten divisions. So far, not one of these is complete—not one.

Germany was to deliver twelve divisions. So far we have nothing but a paper army from Germany.

The British say that their four divisions on the Continent of Europe will not be integrated with anybody else.

All that has happened during the past two years to strengthen Europe's defenses—all that has strengthened Europe—are the American divisions sent over from the United States.

Although these same European nations placed 200 equipped divisions in the field within sixty days after the outbreak of World War II, now the nations of the Continent are contributing less than ten per cent for the purpose of defending Europe.

Thus it is our dollars and our troops which are building up the defense of Europe.

In spite of these, an old woman with a broom could sweep France into the sea.

According to Mr. Hoover, Europeans reason like this. Right or wrong, they figure that if Soviet Russia wanted Europe, she would have overrun Europe any time within the past five years; that the Russians have no taste for inviting American bombers over Moscow; that the Kremlin is now being strained by the centrifugal force of a vast, newly acquired empire.

Soviet Russia just sits and lets the United States carry the burden.

Soviet Russia faces East, because communism's chances are better with the bitter Asiatics.

Then what are we doing in Asia? Our government vetoed General MacArthur's recommendations for using a firm hand; we denied ourselves victory.

We are instead dissipating the resources of the North American continent—the last bastion of real strength in the free world.

We are financing vast armies when it is not our armies but our bombers which hold communism at bay.

While taxes invade our house by the front door, rising prices come in through the kitchen. The purchasing power of our money has decreased forty per cent since the end of World War II.

Lenin once said that the very first step in destroying a government is to debase its currency. We have let the Kremlin goad us into doing just what it wants.

Therefore, Mr. Hoover recommends that we recalculate our risks, and concentrate on keeping ourselves strong.

Therein it seems to me lies the crux of the thing.

We seek peace through strength. That requires we keep us—spelled U.S.—strong and we are as of now way off the beam.

I do not say just boot Europe into the dump heap of history. But I do say, look out for Texas first.

Take a good look at our bank book, because if Texas goes broke it is not going to do the Belgians any good.

Students of prophecy say there will not be a truly United Europe; that the ten pieces of the Roman Empire will not again cleave together.

For two thousand years history has been proving that prophecy right. Since Charlemagne and Napoleon, Louis

XIV and Christian IX . . . and the Kaiser and Hitler . . . all attempts to unite Europe failed.

Today Europe is tired. She is still on her feet but is punch drunk.

Anybody, American or Russian, who tries to make a fighter out of her again will find the battered old Continent more of a liability than an asset.

Spurred by a strong and really sound example, other generations of Europeans may raise themselves and find a new place in the sun.

But by continuing to whip a dead horse, we can expect only to spend our own strength for nothing.

Don't be misled by the good feeling of the false prosperity of war-inflated dollars lest tomorrow's historians write of the United States as Gibbon once did of Rome . . . that their great gift burned brightest . . . as darkness engulfed it . . .

Keep America strong first!

TEXANS LOVE TEXAS

I am going to talk about love.

Webster does a creditable job of defining it in two hundred words.

But the "sex books" have been outselling Webster lately and they are getting us all mixed up.

The perfume ads have us thinking love comes in bottles.

The magazine fiction and radio soap operas make it sound like a mental illness.

It is no wonder that when we tell our youngsters that they should love their God, and their parents, and their flag, and their home, they say "Yeah, I know."

But they don't know.

A man loves his home; it always needs paint someplace; it never has enough closets. But it has been flavored by his favorite pipe and scarred by the spurs of pint-size cowboys; the carpet is a blend of scrubbed spots and puppy hair and love lives there.

He drives through some strange residential district and there is one house in every block he finds exciting. His eyes dance over the sleek lines of a modern home . . . and they rest . . . on the wide, rambling lawnscape of a traditional home.

There is magnificence in the great stone mansion . . . the cottage is cute . . . but none is home. There is something about each he likes to look at, but not necessarily to live with.

Men feel much this way about women. They come in assorted sizes and shapes, and sleek modern lines, and traditional, and cute, and beautiful, and none of which has anything to do with the one girl with whom he feels comfortable and whom he spends the rest of his life learning to love.

Have you ever taken a small boy to a toy store? Did he want something new? Rarely. He wanted another toy car when the nursery is crammed with toy cars. He liked to

look at the whole inventory, but when he chose one . . .
it was the familiar one.

He delights in the animals in the zoo . . . but his love is
wrapped up in the well-worn coat of his own teddy bear at
home.

Love . . . as Webster says . . . is a "particular fondness
for."

Texans love the United States—but one "in particular."

Many of us have figured love is the same everywhere. But
it is not.

So the House half of our Congress used a meat ax on the
appropriation for foreign aid, lopped off a billion dollars.
Unless the Senate softens, we are shortly going to be accused of not loving our neighbors.

Let us understand something. Love has nothing to do with
it.

Sir Hartley Shawcross, President of the British Board of
Trade, recently told the House of Commons that Britain
is going to continue doing business with communist countries and "The United States is just going to have to understand."

When we recently accused Britain of sending Russia jet
engines for aircraft, the reply was that "they were not the
newest type."

Now Sir Hartley says, "rubber is not a military material."
He adds that Britain, the first five months of 1951, did
more than twice the business with Iron Curtain countries

than she was doing with those same countries before Korea.

Let us wake up to this fact: we have a different standard of values in this country than any people anywhere else in the world.

Here in this melting pot of crossbreeds we have a philosophy which says a human life is the most important thing on earth.

We weep when we send our sons to war.

We love differently.

To Sir Hartley Shawcross, bartering in blood is like dealing in any other commodity. Apparently he would sell cannon to kill his own troops in Korea if he could turn a few pounds profit on the deal.

Should an American sell to the enemy, we would jail him. The Allies who are doing the same thing are being rewarded.

Listen, Sir Hartley, this is your best friend telling you— we love you. Americans and British are kinfolks. It is just that sometimes you have to keep even your own in-laws in line.

So I hope an Alabama Congressman named Battle succeeds in pushing through pending legislation designed to cut you off without a nickel of further aid of any kind from this country as long as you swap any goods on his list with any of our enemies.

You are through working both sides of the street. If you are more interested in making a killing in the hardware business than in stopping this Godless malignancy in our midst . . . then you had better know this.

If you want to make this war a strictly business matter count us out, because, as such, it is a very bad investment.

There are an increasing number of Americans ready to accept General Wedemeyer's recommendation that we do not send another American soldier either to Europe or Asia . . . but send guns . . . and let you fight for your own freedom . . . if you really want it.

The Russians would be quite delighted if we should break up housekeeping and they could pick you off like an over-ripe plum.

If you want to make this a business proposition, we would be better off selling you out quick and staying strong ourselves.

You are tired and we are angry and it is obvious that we love differently.

You say we are just going to have to understand. We do understand, Sir Hartley. We do understand now.

Now you understand this: neither you nor anybody else is going to sell us the idea that to love our neighbors requires that we bankrupt ourselves.

Nor will we sell out our sons.

You will fight this war with honor or you will fight alone.

I am for this United Nations responsibility. The ideal of a united United Nations is a good one.

It is not a thing easily accomplished, or somebody would have worked it out a long time ago.

But my first responsibility, whether Downing Street likes it or not, is to my own wife.

I am going to look out for my own wife first; and you look out for your wife.

Then we shall help each other protect our families. As good neighbors, we'll not try to tell each other how to manage personal affairs, but will help each other when we can.

After that we have a responsibility to our community.

Then to our city, then to our State . . . and then our United States.

After that, what allegiance is left over we owe to the world.

But last . . . not first!

ADVICE TO MR. STALIN

In Moscow the sun is rising over Red Square and the Politburo is brushing its collective teeth and shaving its collective cheek and tying its collective tie.

Right after breakfast I would like very much to have a second cup of coffee with Joe Stalin.

You will not hear this message, Uncle Joe, but I rather think you will hear about it. Because it is going to be in the kind of language you understand.

We are told that the Russians invented the electric light and the submarine. You have made it plain, too, that Russians invented the telephone and the radio and the sewing machine and that Russians first learned the secret of the atom bomb and that Russians discovered the North Pole.

I have another "first" for you, Sir. Russians now have a chance to discover America.

Columbus didn't, you know. America has not really been discovered yet.

But there is a chance you are going to. So I am going to tell you what you are going to find when you do.

First, don't judge us by our friends. Do not measure us by England. England is a bowed, bombed-out, compromised, austerity-starved ghost of the nation that once was.

A ghost without pride, dignity, or even too much honor any more.

England is old and mixed-up and tired and scared and depends upon its former place in the sun. A place remembered by Englishmen quite vividly . . . as it never really was.

You have been judging us as an absurd political experiment on the wrong side of the Atlantic. An experiment intended to give people—who should be herded like cattle —freedom to choose, freedom stupid peasants could not understand.

You have appraised our strength and resources from what you have heard from your spies inside our government.

That, Sir, is rather like judging David by the size of his slingshot. A man named Goliath did just that and came tumbling down with a small-caliber hole in his head.

Your agents have not discovered America just because they have got behind our lines in Washington. The American people do not have their real strength in Washington.

Your information is correct, as far as it goes. There is much "wrong" with America.

But if you will stop the Kremlin clock for three minutes, I am going to tell you the rest of the story.

I am going to tell you what's "right" about America.

Then you decide for yourself about trying to add this particular scalp to your belt.

You have heard from Washington, Uncle Joe . . . and what you heard sounded weak.

But wait until you hear from Kokomo.

That is where our secret strength is that nobody has yet discovered. In Kalamazoo and Oshkosh and Corpus Christi and Kokomo.

Remember this, Uncle Joe . . . you have never heard from the United States until you've heard from Kokomo.

If you could get this through your head it might save you a lot of trouble. In this country the people tell the *government* what to do.

It is in the fields and the factories of this country where you find the giants of our time. Some have their shoes off

. . . wading around in the good, green grass roots of this great nation.

Here are America's real bosses; they are the men who grow the food and buy the bonds and run the machines and carry the guns that win our wars.

And there is not one of them who wouldn't deliver a loaded, triggered atom bomb to the Kremlin and drop it on you personally!

When you can understand this, we will understand each other.

Hitler heard of our soft hearts and figured we had heads to match. Do not make that mistake.

You have heard only from Washington. You have not heard from Springfield and Schenectady and Wichita and Waxahachie.

But if you are not careful you are going to be hearing from those places, too.

I don't blame you or your Foreign Ministry for sizing us up as a pushover. You have set one diplomatic trap after another and each time our State Department fell in. You even tried a military trap, and sucked us into that, too.

But what I am trying to say is you have not fooled Kokomo!

You are deterred from attacking us only because of our superiority in oil and A-bombs.

Joe, Oak Ridge is not our strength.

The atom was split in the minds of men from Harrisburg and Berkeley and Omaha and Erie and there is a lot more resourcefulness where they came from.

It is understandable that you should underrate us. We underrate ourselves. Free competitive American capitalism, in less than 200 years, has surpassed all the combined progress of the world for four thousand years before.

Yet we have not kept American capitalism sold even to our own people. The reason is that you came out with a lesser product better advertised.

That is all I had to say. I just wanted to try to explain a few things before you make us mad. I mean "us" . . . spelled U.S.

Because this quiet American with honest grease under his fingernails is one of a strange breed.

He loves leadership. He wants to be led.

But he will not be pushed!

You can outshout our politicians and outsmart our diplomats and outnumber our foot-soldiers . . . but the brains of free men can outproduce you from here to the next election.

And based on the last one . . . look out for Kokomo.

It is not going to do any good for you to bomb a chunk of Detroit, Chicago, Akron, Pittsburgh and New York, for from then on, Mister, you've had it.

Because the bomb hasn't been built, even by us, that can klobber Kokomo.

You see, Kokomo, USA has a hundred thousand counter-parts.

Mr. Karl Marx has convinced you that all men are eco-nomic entities rather than human beings. So you try to measure your advantage over us with mathematics. Don't do it.

The average disorganized American, Uncle Joe, is a free man . . . who lives his life quietly . . . does one job well, loves one woman completely, prays to God, works like the devil, and thinks absolutely nothing of performing a miracle every six minutes.

You still seem sure that this productivity will not go to war with you, that you can juggle the guns and stack the diplomatic deck indefinitely and that every time an Ameri-can Air Force officer dares imply that we should go after you, personally, our bigger brass will pull the rug out from under him.

Well, Joe, that General was from Kokomo. And millions more Americans are getting mad now. Don't push us!

Our sentimentality and softness have been highly adver-tised abroad.

But all it means in language you can understand is this. We are not using the A-bomb against the *Chinese* . . . because we do not believe in avenging a nasty neighbor by kicking his dog!

But I'll tell you something . . . if you do not get your dog out of our yard we are going to knock your house down!

And we are not coming over to help you rebuild it again!

Now, Uncle Joe, you have heard from Kokomo. You can see now why I thought you ought to know.

An American has a warm heart . . . because there is hair on his chest.

CHAPTER VII

Our Greatest Need

MEN WANTED

We have seen what is right with America . . . and also what is wrong . . . how its strength is undermined and how the opportunities it offers are neglected.

Leadership is needed to strengthen that which is right in America . . . and to overcome that which is wrong . . .

Men wanted. Ten . . . stout-hearted men . . . wanted.

Once upon a time there was a man. His name was Joshua.

He had been thrust into the leadership of his people due to the death of Moses. And Moses was a hard man to follow.

Joshua was scared. He was a little man in a big job and he knew it.

Ringed around by pagan enemies—trembling on the borders of the promised land—there was just the Jordan left to cross—but he did not feel up to it.

Yet he was a man on speaking terms with God.

God knew of his fear, and said "Go on, Joshua. Go on across the Jordan. I will be with thee. Only be thou strong and of good courage."

Joshua's strength increased. He said to the officers of the people, you can start celebrating with a big meal right now because we are going to be in the Promised Land within three days.

He promptly had a bridgehead on the other side of the Jordan on the plains of Jericho and the rest of what happened is well known.

Be strong and of good courage, the Voice had said.

Lean on Me.

Today, as rarely before in history, we need strength and courage. But we do not have it.

When we are out of contact with God, the only source of more strength and courage we have to lean on is each other.

We are scared and we do not want anyone around who is likely to recognize it.

If the news is good we go to sleep, if it is bad we go to pieces, but we will not go to work to change it.

That is why I say, men wanted. Stout-hearted men.

Loyal men . . . with the vision to anticipate the pitfalls in the pages of yet unwritten history.

Men who are willing to step out . . . and speak out . . . and, when necessary . . . talk back.

Let us not be afraid of the MacArthurs.

What we need is a few more men willing to sacrifice anything to stand uncompromisingly behind their convictions.

Men who are not for sale . . . at any price!

Not just General Mac.

Give an ear to the voice of the loyal opposition wherever you hear it.

Men with enough fire in them to raise a little smoke are good for us.

English prisons were vile and diseased dungeons until a man named John Howard objected violently.

Florence Nightingale was not a whisper-voiced Angel of Mercy.

She was one of the most stubborn, high-tempered hot-houses of emotion in history. She plagued and bullied government officials until they trembled at the mention of her name.

But she got decent treatment for the sick.

France had a Joe McCarthy in 1939.

The Nazi-Communist fifth column worked together under the Hitler-Stalin pact to undermine the French Army and Air Force. Even the Minister for Air was named as a part of the conspiracy.

France was warned. France had a McCarthy.

His name was de Kerillis.

But he was called an alarmist. His warnings were ignored.

So in the summer of 1940 France, weakened from within, folded up in six weeks.

There was a Karl Mundt in Czechoslovakia.

He sought desperately to reorganize political parties which had ceased to stand for anything, yet were splitting the vote of the patriotic majority.

But nobody would listen; and Czechoslovakia in two days fell from within to a traitorous minority.

After this event many high officials revealed that they had been Communists all the time.

Let us have more stout-hearted men . . . and let us listen to them in time.

We have been on a political pablum diet long enough . . . it is time for somebody to toss us a little raw meat.

Woodrow Wilson said, "We do not need less criticism in time of war, but more. Honesty and competence need no shield of secrecy."

Yet when Edward Nourse dares to say governments can tax and spend themselves into bankruptcy just like people . . . the truth gets him fired.

Louis Denfeld differed with the Administration, and a new Chief of Naval Operations was appointed.

Albert Wedemeyer's 1947 idea for keeping China out of
Communist hands gets censored, snubbed, and side-
tracked.

Our own loyal majority, unaware, overslept.

Milk-fed, mealy-mouthed intellectuals threaten us with
men like MacArthur by calling them "strong men."

Haven't we yet had enough of weak ones?

Andrew Jackson was told to stay south of the Yalu River
once. Then it was the border into Spanish Florida.

But he went across anyway, and stormed two forts.

For good measure he strained our relations with John Bull.
He caught two British subjects doing business with the
enemy and he shot both of them through the head.

President Monroe boiled.

But he did not boil over.

Maybe it was a good thing for Monroe.

Because nine years later Andy Jackson was President.

Let us not be afraid of men who stand for something.
Those who do not usually fall for anything.

Billy Mitchell believed in air power. He charged his
lethargic bosses with everything from incompetence almost to treason. They ousted him, ruined him, and killed
him as surely as if they had broken his heart with their
bare hands.

Ten years later . . . he was posthumously awarded the Congressional Medal of Honor. History had proved he was right.

I wish we had listened to the Swede who tried to warn us before Yalta and Potsdam not to make so many concessions to the Russians.

But we sent the Swede a nasty note, and sent Alger Hiss to Yalta.

Let us start asking why it is some among us say they can see no real statesmanship anywhere on the horizon.

No wonder nobody wants to lead. If he told us the truth, we would stone him. Or, what is worse, we would stand idly by and watch him stoned.

Go on across the Jordan, the Lord said.

Be strong and of good courage. The Promised Land is just across the river. Go on!

I wonder, somehow, if He isn't trying to say that to us now.

But it is going to take men to lead us.

Men who dare to believe in their God and their country and themselves.

A generation of pyramiding regimentation has taken the fire out of us.

We are as cattle.

We are as the old preacher who cautioned the young preacher, "Now, son, there are two controversial subjects you want to steer clear of—politics and religion."

We have lots of building inspectors but few architects left.

Men wanted!

Men!

Who look like men and sound like men and act like men!

For too long we have forced the dissenter to wait out his reward in heaven.

Rare in any age is the man who will dare to think . . .

And believe . . .

And fight for what he believes!

Who will break ranks with the followers and lead.

And, as a great dissenter only recently told our Congress . . .

Do his duty . . . As God gives him the light to see that duty.

The song says, "Give me ten stout-hearted men and I'll soon give you ten thousand."

I'll raise that. Give me ten and I shall show you where you can find the makings of sixty million.

COON IN THE LOG

In the Ozarks there is a saying, "Why pound the log after the coon is gone?"

Sometime ago . . . a good many Americans were ready to give up . . .

Ready to bury the world's last vestige of constitutional liberty beneath a bumper crop of white crosses on a hillside in Korea.

We had almost decided that corruption had eaten away the last degree of human dignity which was the cornerstone of our Republic.

Then . . . half a world away . . . an American lit a candle in the darkness . . . and started home.

And suddenly that candle became a flaming torch . . . shinging so brightly that it illumined the shadows . . . showing all Americans how far we had backslid from the principles of honesty, decency and morality.

From this torch a hundred million other lamps were lit . . . and pride filled our hearts . . . and suddenly we, like him, were marching men . . . who would not crawl again.

Behind a symbol of those things clean and fine and strong which we had thought forever lost . . . there was a rebirth of enthusiasm.

This is not the sunset of civilization . . . this is the dawn.

Let us get back to pounding the log. The coon is not gone!

With our society surrendering to Satan . . . with our very White House doorstep deep in sordid scandal . . . with our sons noisily marching nowhere until their bloody rut became their silent grave . . . and quick or dead, they could not protest . . .

Suddenly greatness was born in the agony of our suffering . . .

A man straight and tall and uncompromising . . . came halfway around the world to speak for them . . . and to bring us back to our senses.

We the people of the United States forced wide the doors . . .

And fresh, clean air flooded our smoke-filled room.

We had been unsure it was worth the fight . . . now we knew . . .

Since the General came home.

When MacArthur left Japan the high and the humble from many parts of the country . . . businessmen, laborers, housewives and students . . . streamed through the narrow streets converging on the Embassy area for one last glimpse of their conqueror and friend.

Never in Japanese history has any foreigner received such a send-off.

Millions lined the road to the airport . . .

Along every inch of that eight miles . . . the road was lined with them.

Their cheers translated said, "May you live ten thousand years."

He waved . . .

And minutes later the great plane with the General and his party took off . . . and for the first time in fourteen years . . . it headed home.

When MacArthur was dismissed a lot of little folks no bigger than you and I got mad.

We got busy and bombarded our own White House with an avalanche of protest. Some said the wrong man had been fired.

Those who stuffed cotton in their ears waiting for the first flash of white-hot anger to subside . . . were still waiting . . . when across America these little Americans prepared the greatest hero's welcome in history . . . for the General some had sought to shame.

The tumult reached a climax with a White House pronouncement . . . "All right . . . all right . . . the ousted General may address a joint session of the Congress of the United States!"

Those who had sought to bury him were trapped into praising him instead.

They were a little like the Cannibal Chieftain who said, "I sure would like to get me a new boomerang, but I can't get rid of this one."

A PRAYER

Almighty God, send us a leader.

A man with his feet planted firmly in American tradition. A tall man . . . with his head above the fog of selfish interests.

Not a common man. This time, God, send us "an uncommon man" . . . a statesman.

We don't deserve him, but send him anyway.

And hurry, please. The hour is late. The candle of freedom burns low.

FEAR AND—FAITH

Caution is instinctive. That is why the deer jumps and runs at the sound of a snapping twig.

The woman never lived who is not anxious about those she loves. It is a healthy and normal part of mother love.

Just as most men are concerned about keeping their jobs.

So being concerned . . . even alarmed . . . about the dangers around us . . . is healthy and normal and right.

But fear is something different.

If we are afraid . . .

If we use up our adrenalin reserve every time we see a black headline . . .

If we chew our fingernails up past the second knuckle every time the Russians sneeze then we are going to knock ourselves out before the fight.

Modern Americans are not spineless.

Most Americans have so much courage they go looking for danger.

But in the wrong places.

Courage is like love. The supply and the demand are equal, but it is the problem of distribution that causes all the trouble.

This current model of fear is something we have been talked into.

We are afraid of the Russians; that is only one symptom.

We are afraid of atom bombs, flying saucers, and men from Mars.

We are afraid of poverty, but more afraid of work.

So we cheat. The way we pad the expense account prepares our sons to throw basketball games with lies about the same size and even to try to cheat their way through West Point.

We follow the leader who promises everything for nothing.

The politicians keep puffing to keep up. Blowing the bubble bigger and bigger and bigger . . . Because they are no more honest and just as scared as we.

I think it is time we start plowing up this bumper crop of fear.

Recently I spoke to the faculty of Purdue University, and I was asked by a gentleman wearing a gray suit and a long face, "What are we going to tell the students?

They are depressed by prospects.

They say they do not like the score.

They see us spawning too many things not worth dying for.

What can we say?"

I have thought about your question since, and I have your answer now.

I am glad your students are worried. That means there is still hope.

Tell them this.

Tell them for a little while it is going to be a little rough on *our kind of Americans*.

We do not like flinching and fearing and phony wars.

We do not like scented notes to the dog-faces in the icy mud of the rice paddies saying, "Mustn't cross the line— that would be aggression."

We are not the kind of Americans who can take getting our teeth kicked out and yet get up fawning with an in- vitation to cocktails.

We do not like the disloyal in our own country running loose to prosper and propagate while the loyal get drafted. There are a lot of things we do not like and aim to do something about.

But as usual, we are running ahead of our uncertain leaders.

Since Molly Pitcher took her place behind the cannon of the Colonies—we the people of the United States have always been front runners.

Since our scouts rode shotgun on the Wells Fargo Stage . . .

Since our women walked beside the Conestoga wagon carrying a few heirlooms and a coop of chickens and a bag of seed . . .

The magnificent majority of Americans has always known where it was going a long time before anybody got word in Washington.

So just keep going . . .

Keep worrying . . . and keep going.

It will take Washington a while . . .

But eventually they will know . . .

I heard once of a storm at sea.

It was a real cork-bobber. One of those winter things which the North Atlantic can churn up where the steamship customers get so seasick that the hope of dying is the only thing that keeps them alive.

One could feel the great engines straining to force the ship into the teeth of the gale. That is the only way to meet a storm . . . head-on.

But it went on so long that finally the passengers were beginning to crack under the strain.

Huddled in the salon without sleep . . . they wept and prayed . . . fearing any moment the ship would come apart at the seams from the merciless pounding of the waves.

Fearing panic, someone sent for the Captain.

When suddenly he appeared in the doorway . . . the hysteria subsided a bit.

He advanced to the center of the salon without speaking.

But in his calm eyes and kindly face there was assurance.

Then he spoke. His voice, like his face, was calm and masterful.

He told them of similar storms through which he and his ship had come. He told them the machinery was in perfect working order. That there was no evidence of strain on the ship. Then a little emotion crept into his voice. Because two-fisted, barrel-chested seamen have a special respect for the Master of the sea. He said, "We will trust in God and our good ship will bring us through."

The people were quiet . . . were almost brave again.

Many had been praying . . . but they had not been believing.

Now they had looked into the face of their Captain and he had explained things and their fears were gone. But it took facts to reinforce their faith.

I assume they rode out the storm, or I should never have heard this story.

If there are storms in the path of our ship of state we can do one of two things.

If they are little ones, go around them.

If they are big ones . . . head into them.

We shall never be able to run away and we should know by now we get hurt when we get hit from the rear.

We have a good ship. She has been through storms before.

She is seaworthy and strong. Her engine is running well and there is power in reserve.

There are the facts. Now pray. And do not be afraid.

For He—not we—is the Master of the sea.

WANTED—A PORTRAIT

I have a commission for an artist—any artist, to paint a new portrait of Uncle Sam.

We have been portraying him as an *old* man.

He's not, you know.

He's just past middle-age as nations go.

He is an uncle, not a grandfather.

We have been thinking of him as an old gent nine parts dead.

Actually Uncle Sam has yet neither the frailty . . . nor the wisdom . . . of old age.

So I am going to describe him as I see him, Mr. Artist.

And, if you can, capture him on canvas.

I want to show him as he really is to the heirs who are trying to bury him.

Paint me a man.

A mixture of many nationalities.

Sandy hair, receding, graying prematurely.

A little overweight.

A barely perceptible scar or so; he has had a few good scraps, you know.

Oh, he was an energetic, unbridled youth!

Born poor, worked hard, got rich.

So quickly and so rich he is still self-conscious about his fortune!

And so seeks, almost with a passion, to give it away.

He was for a while something of a playboy, I guess you'd say.

He's settled now . . . but still self-conscious about success.

Still lacking quite the maturity, the stability to match his station.

He stoops a bit, purposely to appear humble—tips too freely and too much . . .

Bestows gifts beyond good taste.

And so buys mostly envy.

You've a big order here, Mr. Artist. Because I do not want some abstract thing. I want a good, accurate, up-to-date photographic likeness of Uncle Sam.

It is the eyes that will be the hard part.

He must wear the expression of a man who might be figuring a problem in higher mathematics or nuclear physics or listening to the bugle of an Ozarks coon dog—and understands each.

Not a thick-necked, barrel-chested behemoth.

Not all muscles and masculinity. Remember there is some woman in each gentleman.

Maybe this will help—if you see him as a man who is fond of all children.

But who loves his own.

And cannot hide his pride in all they do.

Who would appear least comfortable in dinner dress—uncomfortable in uniform. Most comfortable sitting on the floor fixing a lamp cord with a screwdriver from the car and a paring knife from the kitchen.

A man who is on speaking terms with God.

But we must be honest or your oils will be wasted . . .

His prayers are not generally a kneeling proposition, except in time of trouble.

Usually it is in bed . . . and in silence.

With ample wealth . . . he manufactures fears about his health.

Some ne'er-do-well nieces and nephews have told him how bad he looks . . . that there must be some serious thing wrong with him.

There is not, of course.

But he takes something for it anyway.

He needs exercise more than he needs their habit-forming pills . . .

But he takes the pills.

Well, that's as much as I can tell you about him, Mr. Artist.

He is neither saint nor ordinary.

He's done some good work and had some good times.

There's good stock bred into him and he'll survive a few bad times too.

Paint him serious . . . almost intense.

But with eyes creased by a smile which just left and expects momentarily to return.

Lips . . . full. A good chin . . . with just a hint of another one.

Hands strong . . . halfway to being fists.

I know it's not good to hurry you, Mr. Artist.

But I would like to show such a portrait to his family— while we are all together.

So work quickly if you can. But, above all, paint me a man so true to these specifications . . . that his heirs of today's generation will stop trying to bury him prematurely under a mountain of pills for imagined senility ills. So that they will remember he is still the heavyweight champion of the world. He's not sick, he is not old and he is not retiring!

They've got to see him as he is . . .

A virile, vigorous, versatile, wonderful guy . . .

So that they'll stop waiting for him to die . . .

And loving him . . . help him . . . to live.

CHAPTER VIII

Observations

IF LINCOLN HAD GONE TO HARVARD

What would have happened to the United States if Lincoln had gone to Harvard?

During a recent Lincoln Day, I heard and read many speeches.

The things most of the speakers said did not sound much like the man they were talking about.

I could not help wondering how history might have been written if Lincoln had gone to Harvard.

I use Harvard as a symbol of the caliber of law school he would probably have liked to attend.

But he could not afford it.

Yet what he wrote any school child can quote . . .

But we cannot remember one sentence from this past Lincoln Day.

So I would like to talk to the persons who made those speeches.

If Lincoln had gone to Harvard . . .

Would he have been influenced by the literary concord
. . . the greatest galaxy of writers America ever produced
at one time? Emerson and Thoreau, Longfellow and Haw-
thorne and Holmes?

Then how would he have written the Gettysburg Address?

As it was, his oration of two hundred and sixty-eight words
had only twenty words with more than two syllables.

Here was a lad whose father could neither read nor
write . . .

Reared in a wretched, almost primitive environment . . .

Walked nine miles to school . . .

Scarcely saw anyone—never anyone important.

I am just wondering now . . .

Could it be we are getting too smart in some ways?

When everybody has gone to Harvard who is going to
dig coal and who is going to deliver milk at three o'clock
in the morning? When everybody has gone to Harvard
who is going to put the rivets in our dreams?

We are finding out that seven thousand words do not
make the Atlantic Charter clear to anybody.

Lincoln might have said it in seven words: "We hang
together or we shall hang separately."

"... I was thinking of my son ... hoping the years will be as good
to him as they have been to me."

The sons of America march away without knowing why.

Parents look to our Capitol and get a speech full of "where-ases."

Lincoln might have said,
    "Either we are at war with Communism . . .
      Or we are not.
      If we are not, let us stop shooting.
      If we are . . . let us aim straight."

But that kind of talk is not scholarly . . .

Does not leave any words big enough to hide anything behind . . .

So instead we just say nothing . . . loud.

I wonder if our intellectual spectacles are getting too thick to see through.

When God wrote laws anybody could understand he did not need all those big words.

But we do.

We die without knowing why because we cannot understand each other.

We'll also be hearing Washington Birthday speeches.

There are still a lot of Americans with blood in their veins and hair on their chests and a burning love of liberty in their hearts . . .

So what Washington said should not be translated into double talk.

He said, "Avoid overgrown military establishments."

He said, "Preserve the integrity of the three branches of government."

He said, "Avoid the accumulation of public debt."

He said, "Be alert to the insidious wiles of foreign influence."

If the politicians on Washington's Birthday do not go along with what President Washington stood for . . . let them say so.

But they should not try to draft him as a salesman for some hit-and-miss form of state socialism.

Maybe, these speakers ought to try their words on for sincerity. Instead of for size.

That way even those who do not agree with them will understand and respect them.

We'll all assist them if they talk plain talk and aim straight.

And if they do not feel up to it, they should ask for help.

In the Ozarks they always say a man gets his best aim . . . on his knees.

THREE MEN—ONE FAITH

OTIS

This is the story of three wise men.

Three "other" wise men.

James Otis, born 1725, was a Protestant.

His first tutor was the local minister in West Barnstable, Massachusetts.

Graduated Harvard a plump, pleasant, promising lawyer.

Practiced in Boston until he was noticed by the King, and was made a bureaucrat for the Crown.

As Advocate General, he soon learned what was really expected of him was to authorize snooping for, and rail-roading of, violators of the Sugar Act.

Then something happened inside this hybrid American, and he resigned his lucrative office.

He gave all of his time, talents, and energy to opposing royal invasion of personal privacy.

He raised his voice in behalf of the rights of the Colonists wherever and whenever anyone would listen. When they stopped listening he raised his voice higher.

The once good-humored, sociable fellow had been transformed by a blazing inner fire. The rash, turbulent vehemence of his language distressed even his friends.

But he would not stop.

He became the fiery political leader of Massachusetts Bay.

His pamphlets got him threatened by the King with a treason trial in England.

For he was convinced there must be some better way.

Then one day . . . he made a shouting speech in the British Coffee House at what is now 60 State Street, and officers of the Crown set upon him and administered to him such a beating that he barely survived.

From the blows on the head he was left a ship without a helm.

The drive was still there but the balance wheel was broken.

This man who once, with his brilliant oratory, had swayed the Massachusetts Legislature to oppose the various revenue acts, was stark, raving mad!

Still the fire burned.

In 1775 he broke away from confinement, borrowed a gun, and rushed out amid the flying bullets of Bunker Hill.

Even this he survived.

Until finally this gentle man who had developed a passion for freedom so potent it consumed him . . . in May of 1783 . . . died.

He was struck by lightning while watching a summer thunderstorm.

But James Otis had lived while he had lived . . .

And freedom was conceived.

CARROLL

Charles Carroll of Carrollton was a Catholic.

Born in Annapolis, 1737, his early schooling was with The Society of Jesus.

Eventually he went abroad to study. But most of what he learned in Paris and London was how much he loved Maryland.

There began a determined dream of liberating the New World from the Old. So he returned home and aimed all his efforts at that end.

Barred from politics because of his religion, he became known as "the fighting farmer."

He fought for the freedom of those who denied his.

By 1773 he was the First Citizen of Maryland.

At the Maryland Convention of 1776 it was Charles Carroll whose inspired oratory brought Maryland into line with the other Colonies . . . resolved to break all ties with Britain.

Charles Carroll wanted independence—a truly free country—even before Washington did.

So this man whose religion had denied him the right to vote . . . went on to be elected to Congress from his state and subsequently to the Senate where he served until he resigned in 1792.

In the lower right hand corner of the Declaration of Independence you will see the signature of Charles Carroll of Carrollton.

SALOMON

The third wise man, named Haym Salomon, was a Jew.

Born in Poland, seventeen forty-something. He was never sure. Emigrated to New York in 1772 and became a merchant and did well. Then when the British hired Hessian soldiers to fight the Colonists but could not make their commands understood . . . Salomon could. They hired him as an interpreter.

But he had fought for Polish independence.

His heart was with the Colonists.

He switched signals, and quietly aided the Hessian mercenaries to desert.

In 1776 the British caught on and imprisoned Haym Salomon as a spy.

They said he had plotted to burn the King's fleet and destroy British warehouses.

He escaped.

They caught him again, tried him for treason, sentenced him to death. He escaped.

Went to Philadelphia . . . and went about raising money to rescue the Colonists.

Sick from his confinement in the dread Provost prison, still he labored night and day handling war subsidies advanced by the French and Dutch.

Again and again, at the brink of financial collapse, the cause of the Colonists was rescued by Haym Salomon.

Often alone he contributed the money which maintained government credit.

Out of his own pocket he paid the salaries of government employees and army officers.

Then, one Yom Kippur, George Washington told Robert Morris that the Colonies needed cash from somewhere . . . quickly.

Morris sent for Salomon.

Haym Salomon, his personal resources exhausted, interrupted a synagogue service on this holiest of Jewish holy days to urge . . . finally to demand . . . that the congregation raise the necessary thousands of dollars to loan to the American treasury to meet the emergency.

They met the emergency.

Prematurely, and from the effects of his imprisonment, Haym Salomon died.

Penniless.

But freedom was born.

So goes my story of the three wise men: James Otis, Charles Carroll and Haym Salomon.

Men of three religions . . . one faith.

Notice my choice of words . . . so "goes" the story.

It is not over.

SO YOU ARE GOING TO HAVE A BABY

So you are going to have a baby. A pair never beat a full house, they say.

Mrs. Anna Ranieri was only forty-three.

She had left behind a note which said it all:

"I can't stand this war on my nerves any longer. My brother was killed in Germany and my son in Wonsan, Korea. It is too much to bear now."

They dragged her lifeless body from the cold waters of Lake Michigan.

You do not have to approve to understand.

The page-one miracle of our day is not that some die by way of the window.

The great wonder is that we are not all standing in line for the high ones.

Into such a world you are about to bring a baby.

Next month, maybe.

You are not human if you have not wondered through each long night . . .

If it is right.

Mothers have worried about that since a long time before you switched to low heels.

You'll have to endure the mornings and the waiting and the dieting and the waiting and the wondering and the waiting . . . alone.

But in worrying, you have lots of company.

When Nancy of Kentucky entered the valley of the shadow what was there for her baby? The British were shooting at us in a prelude to war . . .

A former candidate for President and member of the Senate was being tried for treason.

Her husband was an illiterate, wandering laborer.

But in the agony of poverty, war, and public scandal . . . Nancy Lincoln's baby was born.

Suppose you had been Mary, a slave girl.

To you, in Diamond Grove, Missouri, in 1864, it would have seemed the whole mad world was aflame.

Civil war matched the cruel weapons of Grant and Lee.

Sherman was shooting and looting his way to the sea.

Had Mary known that six weeks later she and her boy child would be kidnapped by nightriders and that she would never be heard from again . . . it would not have changed things. She would have had her baby.

For, there were reasons George Washington Carver had to be.

There were important reasons.

We were at war with Mexico when tiny Tom Edison arrived in Ohio.

The day he invented the electric light . . . out in Indian Territory . . . to two worried half-breed Cherokee Indians . . . a boy was born.

He was named Will . . . Rogers.

In Minnesota Edith was frightened, too.

In 1898 the United States was barely struggling to its financial feet when the battleship Maine blew up and the Spanish-American War exploded with it.

At the height of the storm Edith's child was born—Charles Mayo of Rochester.

It was an uncertain adventure for Harry and Catherine Crosby of Tacoma, Washington . . .

Then, too, there was a war to be won.

But more, there was a song to be sung.

And Bing was born.

That is what I am trying to say. That is the whole of it . . .

That there is an important job to do . . .

For a teacher, preacher, mechanic . . .

For a barber, carpenter, doctor, or somebody to grub out the sewers.

It is important.

Even if there are wars.

For it is the soul of man that has to be tried.

An eternity is being populated. Each must test his wings alone . . .

Until he flies.

Then they will take this small world from us and give us the skies.

But we have to be here, first.

That is why what you are about to do is so important.

For each woman there is this personal Garden of Gethsemane.

She goes there for strength.

I have not tried to tell you it is easy . . .

Only that it is terribly important.

None, holding your hand, can erase the terror . . .

Born of the lateness of the hour . . .

And the stories of old women.

Always old ones.

Often childless.

Impatient, tired, you will, of course, be worried.

Since long before Mary, mothers have been anxious for their offspring.

But have borne them in stables and hidden them in bulrushes.

Have borne them unattended in the bouncing bed of a Conestoga wagon racing to outdistance savages . . .

In unheated frontier cabins . . .

Or . . . just as alone . . . midst the antiseptic whiteness of great hospitals.

Because it is important that they do.

It has ever been so!

A while of moonlight and roses . . .

A lifetime of dishwater and diapers . . .

Toys that will not run . . . noses that will not stop . . .

And women . . . back into the garden . . . and again . . .

Barefoot over broken glass . . .

Humming a lullaby.

WHAT ARE FATHERS MADE OF?

A father is a thing that is forced to endure childbirth without an anesthetic.

A father is a thing that growls when it feels good . . . and laughs very loud when it's scared half to death.

A father is sometimes accused of giving too much time to his business when the little ones are growing up.

That's partly fear, too.

Fathers are much more easily frightened than mothers.

A father never feels entirely worthy of the worship in a child's eyes.

He is never quite the hero his daughter thinks . . . never quite the man his son believes him to be . . . and this worries him, sometimes.

So he works too hard to try to smooth the rough places in the road for those of his own who will follow him.

A father is a thing that gets very angry when the first school grades are not so good as he thinks they should be.

He scolds his son . . . though he knows it's the teacher's fault.

A father is a thing that goes away to war, sometimes . . .

And learns to swear and shoot and spit through his teeth and would run the other way except that this war is part of his only important job in life . . . which is making the world better for his child than it has been for him.

Fathers grow old faster than people.

Because they, in other wars, have to stand at the train station and wave good-by to the uniform that climbs aboard . . .

While mothers can cry where it shows . . .

Fathers have to stand there and beam outside . . . and die inside.

Fathers have very stout hearts, so they have to be broken sometimes or no one would know what's inside.

Fathers are what give daughters away to other men who are not nearly good enough . . . so they can have grand-children that are smarter than anybody's.

Fathers fight dragons . . . almost daily.

They hurry away from the breakfast table . . .

Off to the arena which is sometimes called an office or a workshop . . .

There, with calloused, practiced hands they tackle the dragon with three heads . . .

Weariness, Work and Monotony.

They never quite win the fight but they never give up. Knights in shining armor . . .

Fathers in shiny trousers . . . there's little difference . . .

As they march away to each workday.

Fathers make bets with insurance companies about who'll live the longest.

Though they know the odds they keep right on betting . . .

Even as the odds get higher and higher . . . they keep right on betting . . . more and more.

One day they lose.

But fathers enjoy an earthly immortality . . . and the bet is paid off to the part of him he leaves behind.

I do not know . . . where fathers go . . . when they die.

But I have an idea that after a good rest . . . wherever it is . . . he won't be happy unless there is work to do.

He won't just sit on a cloud and wait for the girl he's loved and the children she bore . . .

He will be busy there, too . . . repairing the stairs . . . oiling the gates . . . improving the streets . . . smoothing the way.

CHAPTER IX

Strictly Personal

A DOZEN ROSES

If it's true, and I think it is, that a man does not start living 'till he's married . . . I'll be twelve soon.

There'll be a dozen roses for my Valentine this year.

Some sensible gift—warm if wearable, nourishing if edible; if valuable, negotiable. She'll understand. And a dozen roses.

The day is still a week away, but years timed with a stop-watch have taught me to be everywhere and do everything early. So, as I say, she'll understand.

What does a man remember most about twelve years, when they're gone and the mystery is spent? When he knows what glamour looks like on the ironing board, what does a man remember? Polynesian moonlight through a Venetian blind . . . and cabbage soup.

I remember her a gentle warrior. Tears over trifles, and yet such courage in crises as would have awed King Arthur.

A Phi Beta Kappa key, carefully worn where it wouldn't show. And, in the beginning, soup. Sometimes three days straight.

The beauty of the Bitterroot Valley, Michigan snow, and the Oklahoma Tire and Supply Company at Sixth and Boston. Hard work, in a world so small we had to squeeze into it.

Happy partnership, each too busy rowing to rock the boat. The time we equipped for tennis and Reveille, chasing strays, limped home with puppy pads bleeding from the chase. The tennis balls are Rev's.

The rackets, used only once, gather dust.

This I remember. In memory's black satin casket, these are my jewels.

A book of Browning, bound in hand-tooled leather.

The rose bowl that cost my lunch allowance for a month.

A snapshot of her in a sweat-soaked wallet from the left breast pocket of an army shirt.

Homecoming.

Together we built ourselves a farm. Felt proud a mile deep. Transplanted two family trees. Carpeted a hillside and a house. The house part, hers. Civilized with tile in the bathroom, porcelain in the kitchen . . . and mouse-traps in the basement.

We would retire, I said, while we were young. And we will, for indeed we still are. This thinning hair does not mean what you think. I'll lose it early. Everything early. She'll understand.

My Valentine has some fire in her.

Among her trophies for debate are the scalps of one veterinarian, one child's photographer, and one husband.

She will argue with federal spenders, movie morals, and drugstore scales . . . with some success.

But passive resistance . . . she taught Gandhi.

Selfish? My love selfish? Enough to checkmate selfishness. No more, I think, nor less.

Imperfect? Call it "human." Yes, quite human. Wouldn't it be eerie if she weren't, particularly after dark.

In-laws? I've a million of them. None in politics, in jail, or indigent.

Critical concern for one another; closing ranks on the outsider; folks on speaking terms with God.

And then one day a dream. The valley of the shadow. A miracle. A son. Soft, strong chains.

And yet, he hurries so past youth. Already eager to be somewhere early. So like his dad; she'll understand.

And one day the robin will flutter from the nest, and she'll be mostly mine again.

A dozen roses.

Perhaps this year I'll write a sentimental note. I've not made poems for such a long time now. It won't be very good, but she'll like it. It won't make sense to others, but she'll keep it.

Call it a premium on my best investment.

For of stocks and bonds and real estate and bank accounts . . . she, alone, is all that I can take with me when I die. Though, God willing, I'll go first.

I don't want to be late. And I wouldn't want to wait . . . alone.

She'll understand.

REV

We have talked about the world's larger issues.

By such standards, the life or death of one cocker spaniel dog is of little consequence.

But for seven years Reveille has been a very important part of the Paul Harvey household. A gift from Angel when I returned from the Army, Rev always knew that she was very personally mine.

One man's handful of love wrapped in black fur. Just love. Reveille was almost worthless for anything else. If there is anything else.

Never long on tricks or manners, always scampering on ahead of the family outing, pausing just to look back now and then . . . to be sure we were following.

Our Ozarks farm, Reveille Ranch, is named for her.

She's been my co-pilot on trips there, and shared completely my enthusiasm for green pastures, despite beggar lice, cockleburs, and exhaustion which, at the day's end, sometimes required that she be carried upstairs.

She has shared steak smuggled under the dining table and has fasted with me when family crises made food unpalatable. Adored by Angel, and by small Paul whom she considered a brother.

Reveille had never been told she was a dog and probably wouldn't have believed it, anyway. She was a little girl, very much a member of the family, and owned twenty-five per cent of its voting stock.

Her bed was the foot of my own.

Perhaps at this point I should explain that I am the man you so often see on a city street . . . two hundred plus pounds and six feet two and with the tiniest dog in the block at my side. My feeling for Reveille is just a mite absurd by the standards of sensible folks; I would not pretend otherwise.

Once she was seriously ill.

Previously Angel had been snatched back from the doorstep of death at Chicago's Lying-In Hospital.

The Chief of Staff, Dr. William Dieckmann, I knew as a personal friend.

This hospital, despite its tremendous influx of complication cases, has established a record for "safe deliverance" unparalleled anywhere in the world.

Dare I seek counsel of one of the world's most outstanding gynecologists concerning the ailment of a little dog?

I dared.

My inquiry was not taken lightly. Another examination was conducted promptly, and a date for surgery was set . . . Sunday.

I was there. Drinking black coffee in the room adjacent, while they operated on a small dog in one of the world's great hospitals.

Dr. Dieckmann, his own arm in a sling from bursitis, stood by as consultant to surgeon Dr. J. Garrett Allen.

The chief anesthetist for the hospital was on hand on his day off to administer the very newest in controlled anesthesia.

Two male nurses were in attendance. An expert from Hematology checked a blood sample and arranged for a post-operative transfusion. None among them took this task less seriously than if it had been his most important patient.

Surgery is ninety-two per cent hard, painstaking, time-consuming, exhausting, physical work. When the two-hour-long operation was over, Dr. Allen and I stayed with Reveille until she recovered consciousness. Then watched her until she was out of danger.

I do not believe any amount of money could bring this first-string staff of physicians together for such an operation.

I know they refused any such reimbursement from me.
Nor were they taken away from their duty to other pa-
tients. It was supposed to be their day off.

They gave Reveille, instead, some of those priceless few
hours a doctor reserves for his own family. With those
hours, they bought for Rev and me another year and a
half together.

And now, as I catalogue my memories of those months, I
am very grateful for them. . .

For each noisy greeting, and each sad-eyed good-by.

The tangled handful of brunette in my broken comb.

The times she stood on hind legs—peering over the rim of
the bathtub. And the once she jumped in.

The special game that she taught us, baiting each passing
foot with a strategically-planted tennis ball. Scampering
after it . . . skidding to a stop . . . and prancing back
with her prize in her mouth and her puppy tail geared
to her happy heart.

Or racing away . . . with now and again a nimble pirou-
ette . . . and that familiar quick-glance back . . . to be
sure we were following.

We didn't let ourselves think little Reveille's story would
ever have to end . . . until last December. This, they
said, was not an illness all man's skill could match.

Angel and I hoped and worked and hid the hurt to salvage
small Paul's Christmas . . . and hers.

Before I finish, let me say . . . whenever the pets of others have passed away and my broadcast has been moved to mention them, friends . . . warm, generous, sympathetic . . . have offered the disappointed one another pet to replace the loss.

Please, in this case, try to understand and respect this sincere wish. I will not have another. I don't mean this to sound blunt or ungrateful.

One day, some older, small Paul will have his. But I have had my dog. Her name was Reveille.

She went quietly to sleep at the foot of my bed one recent night.

With flying weather marginal, I took Reveille and a pastor friend, Halvord Thomsen . . . and we drove all night . . . to Reveille Ranch in Missouri.

Rev always loved riding in the car.

And with the dawn still sleeping behind the Mississippi River Palisades, Pastor Thomsen volunteered some gentle words she would have understood . . . and there we buried Rev.

With her favorite ball . . . on her favorite romping ground . . . the hillside lawn which slopes down from the house. The south slope. Rev loved the sunshine so.

And death is like those cliffs across the river; a whole world lies beyond, but hidden to us now . . . from here.

And so I know that warm days and winter snow to come . . . there beneath the sod beside the sun dial . . . with eager, bright-eyed backward glance . . . a small dog hesitates . . . and waits for us to catch up.

ASTOUNDING DISCOVERY

One day the big bell on the porch of Reveille Ranch sent the call to dinner echoing across the fields.

I put aside my work and headed for the house. As usual, I parked the jeep, greased the tools, and went upstairs to bathe.

If I puffed any more than usual on the stairs, I did not notice.

A warm bath, a shave, and some fresh linen later . . .

I faced the mirror for a final backhand with the hairbrush.

Suddenly I stopped short.

I may have cried out a bit; I am not sure.

It was not the face in the mirror which had stunned me. I am used to that now.

But I stood there . . . unbelieving for a long moment.

There was no use pretending . . . no longer any possibility of ignoring the irrevocable, undeniable truth.

The last of the day's sunshine which had been slicing through the Venetian blinds faded as I stood there.

I replaced the hairbrush, turned from the mirror, and started for the stairs.

Nothing would ever be quite the same again.

I knew that now.

Harvey's life . . . all at once . . . was half gone.

Harvey was over the hill.

The hairbrush had told him . . . the hairbrush . . . had hurt.

Harvey was sunburned . . . on top.

So it was that I combed cautiously to conceal the bald spot from a family that probably had seen it coming for a long time . . . and went down to dinner.

The family said the food was delicious.

I thought everything seemed to need salt.

It was sometime later when I sat alone on the upstairs porch, scratching chigger bites on one ankle with the house slipper on the other foot, and looking out across the orchard to the river. I was feeling better.

The sharpness of my awakening had been dulled by my favorite pie for dessert.

So I was in the neighborhood of middle age. After all, there are not a lot of nice people in that neighborhood.

Yesterday I had felt fine. Had spent a whole day in the fields swinging an eight-pound sledge.

Everything was not going to be changed in a few hours just because I had discovered my hair was thin in one spot.

Has not someone once said intelligent people lose their hair faster than most . . . or was it the other way around?

So it was, that while the world was totally unaware of his very personal discovery . . . in the Ozarks the farmer with the fringe on top started counting more carefully his remaining blessings.

What does a man think about when he sees the past stretching out further than the future? When he cannot blame the war or the weather or the State Department?

A man who once laughed at ladies for trying to fight time with cosmetics cannot very well complain aloud now in his own behalf.

I have timed this thing so badly . . . so very badly. Television on the way in at the same time my hair is on the way out.

But that is not really what I thought about as I sat there on the porch.

I was thinking of my son . . . hoping the years will be as good to him as they have been to me.

I was very glad for the patch of green and the bit of blue that is mine on this hilltop in the Ozarks. For here in this good earthy place my family will always "belong."

You know what I mean?

This is my land. I have watered it with my sweat and fertilized it with my footsteps.

Here, as long as time exists, I will be warm every winter and young again . . . every spring.

Jesus understood a man's need for pride in that which is his own, when he told us not to covet that which is our neighbor's!

We hill folks are not very intellectual about some things, but one gets mighty close to the truth with his hands in the soil of these foothills of Heaven.

A man has to belong someplace.

Whether it is a fifty foot front on a city street or a half acre in the suburbs, a man has to belong.

You do not find many homeowners in jail.

A man with grass to cut and back steps to fix hasn't time for any detours.

The American dream was made real by men who wanted to belong. ———— — —— —— ——

Any government that seeks to take away or tax away the personal property of the individual . . . at once or by degrees . . . that government is bad and wrong.

Maybe this will make it more plain.

The tree in your yard is yours. The fruit a gift of Divinity. If you want to eat it, can it, sell it, or give it away . . . that is your privilege.

The government should have no interest other than to expedite the process. The government's responsibility is to guard your trees from being harmed or your fruit from being stolen.

In exchange for such service, the government has a right to exact a fee or tax. But the service should be rendered as such and at cost.

When the government comes into your orchard and tells you to pick your fruit . . . then the government takes it and sells it . . . or gives it away for the purpose of winning political friends . . . then the policeman has turned thief.

And Uncle Sam, himself, becomes a fence . . . dealing in stolen goods.

We have strayed a considerable way from this fundamental right of ownership in the quarter century I vividly recall.

I guess that is all I had to say.

Nothing earth-shaking is happening out at the ranch. Small Paul is pacing the floor outside the hen-house door. Baby ducks are due any day now.

The apples are ripening round and red.

The birds are awake while the morning is still asleep so the sun can come up to music.

As I said . . . nothing earth-shaking. Just a little loafing and a lot of living and a miracle every seven minutes.

Maybe I could see more clearly now because there was less hair in my eyes.

Or maybe it's because my library was mostly back in Chicago and I went right to the hill folks for my answers.

They are not asking anything for nothing. They'll grow their own meat and potatoes and make their own gravy. But they have one bad habit . . . they just will not lock their doors.

To us, for whom life is half done, it will not matter much.

But one day may others belong to these green acres . . . because we deserved them . . . because we fought all enemies to preserve them . . . all enemies . . . foreign and DOMESTIC.

Lock the door. Oil the shotgun over the mantel. And stay aware!

For the new enemies of American freedom pose as friends bearing gifts.

Now, my learned contemporaries of high degree . . . I am aware that my recommendations for hanging onto our Republic with both hands circumvent most of your geopolitical considerations.

You speak for the architects . . . I'll speak for the builders . . . the men who can straighten rusty nails and build all this all over again.

Here in the hills and plains are the builders . . . wherever their towers rise.

And to know them is to understand why God so often chose the simple ones . . . to confound the wise.

Printed in the USA
CPSIA information can be obtained
at www.ICGtesting.com
CBHW071136150424
PP15090600001B/11